THE PLANT THIEVES

PRUDENCE GIBSON is an author and research academic in plant studies at the School of Art and Design, University of NSW. She is lead investigator of an Australian Research Council project on the National Herbarium of NSW. She is the author of *The Plant Contract, Janet Laurence: The pharmacy of plants* and *The Rapture of Death*, and is a contributor to the *Sydney Review of Books* and *The Conversation*.

'*The Plant Thieves* is a real treat. I found myself intrigued, amused, surprised, occasionally infuriated, but always engaged and provoked. Prue Gibson's discursive tale of Sydney's herbarium beautifully intertwines art and science, and boldly tackles the gnarly questions of decolonisation and equitable sharing of information. A must-read for anyone interested in plants and plant collecting (or is it thieving …).'

TIM ENTWISLE

'This reads like a Michael Pollan book with a feminine touch! Prue tells the hidden and too-often silenced stories of our past and present relationships with plants, inspiring hope for the future. Highly recommended.'

MONICA GAGLIANO

'This book will take you on an adventurous read through the lives of plants and their people. It is scholarly, personal and surprising, reflecting the writer's deep curiosity and love for plants.'

JANET LAURENCE

'Very rarely do herbaria come alive and tell stories with so much vividness as in this book by Prue Gibson. Through her sensitive writing and attentive engagement with plants, we encounter them face-to-face, face-to-surface, surface-to-surface, and travel further along to the worlds they once moulded and were part of.'

MICHAEL MARDER

'Wonderful stories that bring to life vegetal treasures & their fraught histories within the colonial herbarium. A journey that creates fascinating human and plant connection.'

CAROLINE ROTHWELL

'Gibson threads the personal through the botanical in this stunning book about ecology, humanity and the future of our world.'

ANNA WESTBROOK

For Thomas, George and Evie

Also by Prudence Gibson
The Rapture of Death (2010)
Janet Laurence: The pharmacy of plants (2015)
The Plant Contract (2018)

As editor
Aesthetics After Finitude (2016)
Covert Plants (2018)

THE PLANT THIEVES

| Secrets of the herbarium | PRUDENCE GIBSON |

NEWSOUTH

A NewSouth book

Published by
NewSouth Publishing
University of New South Wales Press Ltd
University of New South Wales
Sydney NSW 2052
AUSTRALIA
https://unsw.press/

© Prudence Gibson 2023
First published 2023

10 9 8 7 6 5 4 3 2 1

This book is copyright. Apart from any fair dealing for the purpose of private study, research, criticism or review, as permitted under the Copyright Act, no part of this book may be reproduced by any process without written permission. Inquiries should be addressed to the publisher.

A catalogue record for this book is available from the National Library of Australia

ISBN   9781742237688 (paperback)
        9781742238722 (ebook)
        9781742239668 (ePDF)

Internal design Josephine Pajor-Markus
Cover design Regine Abos
Cover image Preserved specimen of *Acacia phlebophylla*, F.Muell. ex H.B.Will., Buffalo Sallow-wattle recorded on 1913-01-18. Image provided courtesy of the Royal Botanic Gardens and Domain Trust. Digital specimen image from the National Herbarium of NSW, accessed on 28 November 2022 from https://registry.opendata.aws/nsw-herbarium.

All reasonable efforts were taken to obtain permission to use copyright material reproduced in this book, but in some cases copyright could not be traced. The author welcomes information in this regard. This work contains Indigenous Cultural and Intellectual Property and is used with consent of Traditional Owners. UNSW Press supports the United Nations Declaration on the Rights of Indigenous People, including article 31, which states that:

Indigenous peoples have the right to maintain, control, protect and develop their cultural heritage traditional knowledge and traditional cultural expressions, as well as the manifestations of their sciences, technologies and cultures, including human and genetic resources, seeds, medicines, knowledge of the properties of fauna and flora, oral traditions, literatures, designs, sports and traditional games and visual and performing arts. They also have the right to maintain, control, protect and develop their intellectual property over such cultural heritage, traditional knowledge and traditional cultural expressions.

FOREWORD

Plants are not green wallpaper, a backdrop to the environment, and are not something that can be removed without critical impact. They of course absorb carbon dioxide and release oxygen, they provide habitat and food for all components of biodiversity and provide a legacy for the future. But because we downplay them, even disregard them, too often we do not include them in mitigation programs and, worse, continue to remove them from landscapes.

We face the risk that a substantial cohort of plants that are not yet formally recognised, at least from a conventional scientific perspective, will perish before this process can be completed. It is currently estimated that up to 40 per cent of plant species are at risk of extinction through land clearing, the impact of invasive species (weeds, insects and diseases) and of course the suite of impacts caused by climate change. As we have seen only too clearly with the 2019–2020 Black Summer fires and the east coast floods in 2022, erratic weather patterns mediated by climate change can have vast and dramatic effects on the ability of species to survive, reproduce and thrive.

Billions of plants were annihilated, or impacted severely, in the Black Summer fires, their survival dependent on tiny seeds stored in the soil protected from the heat, or in the case of some species, in buds under a protective coating of bark. This survival is dependent on a fire-free period over the next five to ten years, but the long-term projections do not offer surety on this front.

There is an essential need to reconnect with plants, to understand better how to protect them, cherish those that already exist, and learn how to restore and regenerate degraded, damaged and destroyed landscapes in a way that will be truly sustainable and resilient. We have already damaged far too much of the planet and are on a one-way path to living with substantial levels of temperature rises. This will change the paradigm in which we need to restore landscapes and we may need to accept approaches to species and provenance selection in order to choose plants that will survive and remediate rather than specific local provenances. This will challenge many of us working to restore ecosystems and save species and ecological communities.

We clearly need to learn from Indigenous peoples and to work with them to harness tens of thousands of years of knowledge in the remediation of landscapes and apply them to the management of ecosystems to protect communities, infrastructure and biodiversity. For too long we have dismissed the accumulated knowledge built up over millennia by Aboriginal peoples, not recognising that it is based on true scientific foundations of observation and experimentation and that it possesses enormous amounts of information that we should be applying to solving the issues at hand.

This information and knowledge should also be reflected in how we name and describe the flora, fungi and fauna that we live with, using genus and species epithets based on Indigenous language words (with appropriate consultation and approval). There is much that can be done to decolonise science.

The combination of science and art also offers new ways to interpret the complexity of science. Botany and plants in general have always inspired art and there are now opportunities to incorporate all aspects of art and media in new ways to interpret the complexities of the plants. Art can shine a light on plant blindness and underscore the importance of plants in dealing with both the climate and biodiversity crises.

This book arose out of a collaborative project ('Exploring Botanic Gardens Herbarium's Value, via Environmental Aesthetics') between Dr Prudence Gibson and Dr Sigi Jottkandt at the University of New South Wales, Professor Marie Sierra at University of Melbourne, staff (including myself) at the Royal Botanic Gardens and Domain Trust as well as the Bundanon Trust, that was funded by a grant from the Australian Research Council's Linkage program. This project initially aimed to explore the aesthetics of the priceless collection at the National Herbarium of New South Wales. The herbarium has just moved to a new facility at the Australian Botanic Garden, Mount Annan, and has been digitised with the vast majority of specimens photographed at high resolution. Our project has explored much more than that – examining how people value (or don't) plants, the myriad uses of plants and the critical importance of plants to humanity's future. This book provides a great opportunity to reflect on these aspects from a range of perspectives and how we might all begin to centre plants in our daily life.

Brett Summerell
Chief Scientist and Director of Research
Australian Institute of Botanical Science
Royal Botanic Gardens and Domain Trust

CONTENTS

Introduction	xv

PART ONE First encounters

Meeting the herbarium	3
Meeting my first herbarium specimen	6
Luke and the banksia	14
Joseph Banks in the herbarium	19
Two-way botany	25
Zombie fungus and the black drink	30
The ugly hornwort	35
'Barbara is amazing'	42
Discovering the monster	46
Uncle Ivan	55
Lifeblood: Aunty Susan and Natalie	60
White death	65
Denise and the black bean	69
Dieffenbachia and the Himmler story	76

PART TWO Psychoactive plants and their keepers

The cacao ceremony	87
Who can access the plants?	92
Colonised by the plants: psychoactive cacti gardens	99
The psychoactive gardens visit	103
The oldest psychoactive garden	108

The cactus fail	113
Fungi fever	116
Psychoactive wattle	124
Darklight and the whole point of the thing	132
The plant thieves and the secret species	135
The herbarium acacia	136
Psychotherapy	139
Plant drug legislation	142
Biosecurity and Shelley's broken wrist	150

PART THREE Rewilding, conservation and creative revaluing

The wild banksia woman and rewilding debates	161
The missing daisy and lost species	166
Fast evolution	173
Bioprospecting and the African olive trees	178
The African olive tree	182
Hardenbergia and the witches forest	187
Violence and murder	192
Labyrinth	196
Collecting is a curse	199
Plant blindness	202
Cathy Offord and the Wollemi	211
The plant artists	216
Dakota and the flame tree poem	222

The plant smells of memory	229
The rights of plants	238
My mother and the orchids	242
The banksia: plant-spirit	245
Acknowledgements	249
Notes	251

I acknowledge the Traditional Custodians of this unceded Country and their cultural plant knowledge spanning over 60 000 years. I write this book from Gadigal Country, the land now known as Sydney, New South Wales.

First Nations readers are advised that this work contains references to people who have passed away.

INTRODUCTION

Who gets to tell the stories of plants? Who gets to collect them? Name them? Describe them?

This book is inspired by the National Herbarium of New South Wales. The herbarium was established in 1853 and has a collection of 1.4 million plant specimens that are dried, mounted and stored. It is a place to protect plants, to conserve, restore and memorialise them.

But what are the stories of those plants? Where did they come from? How were they collected? By whom? Why is access to some plants restricted? How can fragile species be protected? And why is there so little acknowledgement of Indigenous plant culture in scientific institutions?

While the herbarium's collection is romantic and rich, it is also the epitome of the colonialist fervour to collect and dominate nature. Part of the inextricable relationship between plants and colonialism is all the theft, all the death and all the control exerted over land and First Nations peoples that are part of Australia's history.

This story of pillage and theft within botanical history is the challenge for the herbarium. It is a place of exquisite beauty and holds seeds and secrets of future life. But it also records the violence and damage done to the earth, the trees, the plants and to the very future it promises to secure. It is this paradox of taking versus keeping that makes the herbarium endlessly interesting.

And, as I discovered, there are also those outside the herbarium working to preserve plant species – in some cases plant thieves becoming plant protectors.

This project began when I applied for a three-year grant to collaborate with the National Herbarium of New South Wales at Sydney's Royal Botanic Garden. My application asked how art and narrative could revalue plants, and the grant from the Australian Research Council gave me three years to find out a few more things about plants: What are they? Who are they? *Which one is mine?*

The quest initially was to make better sense of our human relationships with plants, to face the truth about colonial erasure of Indigenous knowledges about plants, to learn about conservation and to better understand psychoactive plants. I am driven to know more about plants and also more about plant people. Over the three years of the project, I spoke to botanists, horticulturists, genetic researchers, conservators, artists, poets, Traditional Owners and historians to find out what human–plant relations really are and what they mean. And what that meaning tells us about the herbarium.

At the time, it crossed my mind that there might be a plant out there that could be my own spirit-plant, a plant that had a particular connection to me. I realise there are complexities around this fundamental urge I have to connect with a plant. There is the risk of it being perceived as appropriation or mimicry but much of my own heritage regarding clan-plant associations is lost. My grandparents and father are no longer alive to share this cultural information with me. But I have a drive, which feels deep and timeless, and it propels me to build a relationship with a particular plant. It's a risk I'm prepared to take.

This story is about diving into the plant archive of the herbarium as a way to kick off my search for more plant knowledge, but also as a way to ground my quest in the physical matter of the archival documents. Archives are materially present. The story is also a celebration of all the plant people I have met. It is a documentation of how the artists and poets I commissioned to respond to the herbarium through their creative practice showed me things I couldn't previously see.

Once you see plants for who they really are, you can't unsee them or unknow them. Seeing creates change. I guess the question is whether you want to be changed by plants too – but it might happen anyway, with or without your permission.

When I started writing, the National Herbarium of New South Wales was located within the Royal Botanic Garden in Sydney. When I finished the book, the collection of plants had been photographed, packed up and moved to a new building at the Australian Botanic Garden, Mount Annan.

Both locations are blissful. The former location was a 1980s building in the heart of the luscious Royal Botanic Garden in the Domain. The latter is a world-class facility in a beautiful rammed earth building set on the hills between Camden and Campbelltown. The herbarium, as I will refer to it, gave me an insight into how a plant institution works, how plants are named and kept, and how botanical history is made. I learned that the herbarium is more than an archive, more than a storage unit. It's a repository for stories – stories about people, as much as plants.

PART ONE
FIRST ENCOUNTERS

MEETING THE HERBARIUM

It's tricky to convey why the herbarium is so exciting. It's like being asked to define 'love' or 'happiness'. The attraction might lie in the way humans are hardwired to classify and order things. Or do we all secretly want to become plants in the wormy earth, reaching for the sun?

The herbarium is a storage place for dried and pressed plant specimens collected from their habitats. It is used for research (historical, evolutionary, climate and genetic) and often involves the sharing and movement of valuable specimens between herbaria around the world to ensure their safety. For example, the herbarium has 1.4 million specimens and the collection is currently worth $280 million.

We need plants for food, medicine, shelter, clothing, culture and wellbeing. The specimens in the herbarium collection record those uses and they also reflect the process of collecting and caring for plants. The sight of so many plant specimens in the herbarium archive is dizzying.

Each specimen sheet, seed collection and spirit jar tells the story of the collector, the place the specimen was taken (including GPS data and habitat details) and any notes recorded alongside official stamps and data. The herbarium follows colonial procedures of naming and classifying plants according to the Latin-based Linnaean system.

The specimens rest inside red archival boxes. Within each box are several manila-like cardboard folders. Inside each folder is a sheet of A4 paper to which the dried plant specimen is attached, usually by tiny white tape. Any seeds or leaves that have fallen off are placed in a small plastic bag and also taped to the sheet. The specimen sheets are not static or completed or resolved, as there are often typed or handwritten notes or stickers explaining previous information. Botanists continue to add up-to-date data. The herbarium is full of rows upon rows upon rows of data. It is a curious, even eerie, place of corridors and shelves, boxes and folders. Eerie because although the plants are inert, they are alive with stories.

In the herbarium, there is the low hum of dehumidifiers, air conditioners and the buzz of overhead lights. But it still recalls the original *wunderkammers* or 'cabinets of curiosity' that were set up to showcase natural objects collected from around the world (which sometimes included fakes). The idea was to create an entire world of miniature exoticisms to remind humans of the vastness and immense variety of nature.

These *wunderkammers* began in the sixteenth century with collectors such as the Austrian Emperor Prince Rudolph II, who collected hundreds of mathematical instruments, coins, Indian curiosities, coral, precious stones, uncut diamonds and paintings. Such collectors often displayed their loot in 'wonder rooms' of curious artefacts and specimens from distant lands.[1] The nineteenth-century collector Augustus Pitt Rivers now has a museum in Oxford, England, in his name, which houses the multiple weapons, magical objects, cultural items including boomerangs, shrunken heads and masks that he collected. Such collections – inspired by expansionism and nationalistic fervour – resulted in colonial legacies that are uncomfortable. The shrunken heads have at last been removed from public display at the Pitt Rivers Museum.

Begun out of ardour for the natural world, the *wunderkammer* evolved during the nineteenth century into more zealous scientific classification and documentation projects.

Collecting examples of the natural world from faraway places was also an act of imperial dominion and colonial exploitation, establishing the colonising countries as masters. It was at exactly this time that the Sydney herbarium took shape.

The herbarium has been considered a wondrous and elegant legacy of colonial collecting, but botany has had a chequered history. For example, women were allowed to participate in the early nineteenth century, only to lose that right when the botanical societies decided information about plant reproduction should not be made plain to womenfolk.[2] But, put aside the misdemeanours and it becomes possible to discover the beauty of the plant collection. It's possible to hear the stories of the botanists and horticulturists, the conservators and geneticists who work at the herbarium. It's even better to hear the stories of the plants themselves, speaking up from their specimen sheets, from inside the herbarium drawers.

The very first specimen sheet I saw surprised me.

MEETING MY FIRST HERBARIUM SPECIMEN

The first specimen I was introduced to was the kelp, one of the sea's algae. When the herbarium box was opened and the paper folder lifted out, I could swear I smelled the ocean. Biting, salty and somehow smelling like preserved lemons. I was surprised because there, in the archive, in the box, filed within a folder, pressed on a page, was an object that transported me to swimming spots I'd known.

Old kelp specimens look a little bit translucent because they have been flattened out in the process of preservation. Kelp loses its sinuous hair-like swaying and becomes more like a blobby sea monster. This particular specimen had tiny spikes in between its arms (branches) and had a little shrivelled-up root at the bottom. There was something sad and beautiful about this kelp.

I'd seen plenty of photographs and scans of specimen sheets before I first visited the herbarium collection in its home at the Domain, but I'd never seen one face to face before. This first visit was in 2019, when the director of the Royal Botanic Garden, Kim Ellis, gave me a tour of the facilities. He showed me the drying room, spirit room and the herbarium archive area. The drying room was adjacent to the loading dock, and the field vehicle, a troopie, was parked under cover. Specimens were unloaded from the troopie, dried inside clamped newspaper sheets and spongy foam, then taken to the freezer room before being mounted on the specimen sheet with all the relevant data. And stored. There is a special extra freezer room where all the type specimens (like a first-edition specimen) are kept, along with rare and significant collections.

Kim then took me to the spirit collection room. This is where larger fruits that can't be pressed on a page are stored in alcohol solutions in small to large jars. Kim paused at the heavy door before opening it and said, 'I should warn you that most of the staff think this room is haunted.' Now, as someone who has written a book on death, including chapters on ghosts, monsters and zombies, I am open to different belief systems and more likely to believe things until they are disproven, rather than the other way around.

Even so, it's possible I had a startled expression. Kim laughed and said the reason is that the door often rattles as a result of the hundreds of jars inside altering the air pressure as the alcohol solutions evaporate, change and escape.

Whether or not he was winding me up, I immediately held tight to my notebook as though I was about to be blown away by potent gases. Once inside, there was a strong smell of chloroform-like solutions and rotten fruit, but no spectres. Just hundreds of bottles filled with creepy natural specimens that looked like they would serve well in a horror movie.

After a bit more of a tour, I left the herbarium that day, changed. I honestly had no idea about all the work that went on behind the scenes. As I researched over the next three years, I would find out a lot more about botanical work and the stories hidden within the archive. These stories whispered to me from the edges of the traditional botanical world. There is an overarching story of how plants hold power over humans, if you just care to see how this is so. It was even suggested to me that humans have been colonised by plants, rather than the other way around. I would hear a full circle of stories about plants, and of our futures with them.

As I left that day, I considered whether kelp might be my 'spirit-plant'. Instinctively, I knew it wasn't, but I remained intrigued by it.

*

After meeting kelp at the herbarium, I decided I'd better find out more about this slippery algae, whose shape reminded me a little bit of my own head of hair. I wanted to move beyond the specimen sheet on the page and remind myself what that archival object meant back in the real watery world. What was the relationship between the archival document and the same plant in its environment?

Not long after that visit to the herbarium, a friend posted an image of algae from down at Bondi on Instagram. Both these experiences made me viscerally remember how I detested that golden kelp (of the algae family) at North Bondi, where my father took us swimming most Sundays back in the early 1980s. Both slimy and sharp, the kelp turned my stomach and I would duck-dive away from the floating stuff, kicking at it if it touched my toes. Looking at those Instagram images, I wondered if I would feel the same way about kelp if I got a bit closer to it now.

So I went down to Clovelly, a Sydney beach close to Bondi. I stepped down from the concrete promenade towards the clear, clean ocean water. The chatter and laughter of sunbakers was a pleasant but distant din as I wriggled my toes on the slippery steps.

On this October day the Clovelly water was deep, and it was cold. The temperature outside was a sunny 23 degrees but the water was 16 degrees (and felt like eight). There were loads of people lying on the two deep promenades that flank the channel of water, but only a few people were braving the drink.

I was determined to snorkel and become reacquainted with the golden kelp forests of Sydney's foreshores. My colleague at the University of NSW, Professor Adriana Verges, is an expert in another seaweed, crayweed (also of the algae family). Adriana assures me it is common to despise the slimy touch of seaweed in the ocean, and equally common to become more interested in how algae is critical to underwater biodiversity. She also tells me that crayweed reproduction is not dissimilar to the human version – male sperm to female egg.

The water rushed around my ankles and threatened to yank me in faster than I wanted. Trying to urge my body to move, I stayed rigid. I clung to the handrail near the bottom rung of steps, unmoving. The combination of goosebumps and sun-speckled water turned my legs the same pattern as my swimmers: camouflage. With a deep breath, I pulled on my goggles-plus-snorkel and plunged down into that watery world.

The cold seized the back of my neck and jaw; painful, almost paralysing. I could hear my breathing, strained and heavy. I focussed on the measure of inhaling and exhaling. Then time stretched and the muffled life above water receded and slowed. I kicked through the body of silky space. I hadn't snorkelled for over 20 years: the last time was soon after an attempt to learn deep-sea diving. Still recovering from a decade of intermittent bronchitis, I couldn't seem to conquer the oxygen tank, failed the test, and had to snorkel near the surface while the rest of the diving group disappeared into the true depths.

Snorkelling today became OK. My breathing slowed even more and soon the cold Clovelly water was a chamber of briny allure. The water was silky and my hair felt satiny as it wafted against my cheek and was then tugged back. Waft and tug, waft and tug.

Breaststroking into the channel's centre at the mouth of the beach, I put on my metaphorical lab glasses and began to consciously observe. There! My kelp was there in clumps among the rocks, which brought to mind the kelp specimen sheet in the herbarium and how the rubbery leaves took up almost all of the paper. After leafing through so many specimen sheets, it was easy to stop at the kelp because it looked like dirty water had been spilled on the page.

The cloudless day painted the kelp a golden green. Even five metres away from the closest forest clump, it was not so much slimy as cactus-like. The rest of the kelp across the floor of the bay lit up as my eyes adjusted. Each grouping waved its golden locks at me, moving in sync with the ocean current like ballroom dancers moving in time with an orchestra.

Adriana, preeminent crayweed scientist, is responsible for the strong populations of seaweed along the Sydney coastline. She has been working on seaweed restoration projects since 2010 and has been able to grow substantial new populations after sewage caused a complete absence of algae during the 1970s and 1980s. The new crayweed reproduce fast, according to Adriana. For her first trials, she used huge water tanks to keep the algae in water while they attempted propagation. But the submerged plants failed. So, she dried the crayweed before separating out the male and female (she needed lots of both) before replanting.

As I struck out on my observation mission, froglike, to the deeper water, my hair tugged back and comforted the back of my neck so that I felt at one with the kelp. I glanced down and saw how purple some algae was. It was lichen-like and crawled all over the rocks below. It occurred to me, as I adjusted my smile into more of a pout to stop water sneaking into the snorkel, that because the goggles completely covered and suctioned my nose, that I had no sense of smell. There was no intense, salty, brine smell.

Maybe the lack of smell made everything sound louder: my respiration and the rush of waves against the northern rocks. Yet while the currents were strong, and the waves moved in swirls and rolls, there was a host of fish in front of me that seemed immobile. They all faced south and weren't wagging their tails or shimmying in any direction. They hovered in the water. They were Māori wrasse, but I didn't have a clue what they were doing. I swam closer to take a look.

Below the wrasse were some larger fish. One had slippery blue-grey skin. It was one of the gropers. This beach is famous for its blue gropers. There was an especially large male groper that lived among the kelp forests nearly 20 years ago. When a spear fisherman killed it, there was a public outcry. My sons told me the murdering fisherman was bashed by locals, but I couldn't find any official confirmation of this. The blue groper beneath me was more silver than grey but he was also shadowed by rocks and kelp. I reached out my hand and considered swimming down to touch him but knew better and respectfully moved to deeper water.

After 30 minutes, the cold started to make me jittery and, even though I wanted to stay in, I headed back to the stairs, recalling what Adriana had told me: after they had propagated the crayweed, they had to put it back in the ocean. To keep the algae in place, they drilled large sheets of plastic mesh over the rocks and tucked the holdfasts (the base of the seaweed) between plastic and rock until they affixed. After the seaweed took hold – maybe nine to 12 months later – she and her team removed the plastic. Her restoration project has been enormously successful, with major new algal communities up and down the beaches.

I yanked off my snorkel and goggles and dunked my head a few times, then stepped back up onto the rocks near the exit stairs. Once I was back up on the warm concrete promenade I reached for my towel and tried not to shiver uncontrollably. I texted a friend, a Clovelly local, to ask whether the fisherman-bashing story was true. She replied to say she didn't know but instead told me that when a male blue groper dies, a female in the group changes sex and turns blue! Equally interesting information.

I later found another specimen sheet in the herbarium: the *Seirococcaceae phyllospora* (crayweed). Some had been collected for the Sydney herbarium around 1898 and 1900 along Bondi Beach; one was collected in 1996 at Policeman's Rock on Norfolk Island, and some from along the coast of East Gippsland in Victoria. Specimens were collected in Collaroy and Cronulla during the 1940s. Some include the holdfasts and some do not. Probably the most interesting one was collected by Joseph Maiden in March 1898 from Lord Howe Island. Maiden became the director of the Botanic Gardens in 1896 and was responsible for setting up the herbarium, so this would have been one of his very early collected specimens.

The crayweed specimens in the collection are different from the kelp. Where kelp is wide and almost golden still, the crayweed is more tentacular. The crayweed have long central axes to their branches and the specimens in the herbarium include the crayweed conceptacles. Conceptacles! What a word. It refers to the little blob cavities that contain the crayweed's reproductive organs.

What I love about the crayweed specimens is that they can barely fit on the paper sheets. They give the impression they are trying to break free from the white tape so they can get back to the ocean to continue their swaying. Unfortunately some of the specimens have been cut back to the tiniest piece, perhaps to contain the uncontrollable appearance of the seaweed. I find these tiny, spiderlike specimens (such as the one collected from Policeman's Hat on Norfolk Island) to be a little disappointing, as if they have been hacked to such a small size simply to make them more manageable. For someone who used to hate the sensory touch of seaweed, I now wish all the kelp and other algae in the herbarium collection were free to be back in the sea.

Art has the capacity to make me see real life with fresh eyes. I often think, Oh, the sky looks like a Turner painting. Or, That traffic scene reminds me of a Jeffrey Smart painting. In the same way, the specimen sheets of kelp and crayweed, artforms in their own ways, made me pay better attention to the algae in real life.

LUKE AND
THE BANKSIA

Imagine a young boy, eight or nine years old. Dark, curly hair bobs about his ears. He runs with his cousins along the bush tracks of Kurnell at Kamay, known by many as Botany Bay. This little boy is full of life and the freedom of running barefoot among the coastal bushland.

There's bracken and rainforest plants alongside angophoras and blueberry ash. There are flannel flowers that bloom after bushfires and the currawongs sing and the kookaburras laugh at the majestic white sea eagles.

The boy's name is Luke and he's in the process of starting war games with all his cousins. The idea is to grab all the banksia cones (the rough hard ones with dried brush spikes) and make several ammunition piles. Both Luke's mum and his dad are local Kurnell people and both are Aboriginal. His mum is a sheetmetal worker and his dad is an oyster farmer. His grandma is very politically active, and vibrant with it. He has aunties and uncles living close by, so there's heaps of cousins to have wars with.

Luke is running around grabbing the cones and once the kids are all done with collecting, they pause to assess the situation. Then they set up their base camps, and choose the teams. The piles of banksia cones are not even, so they redistribute them because, as Luke says, it's no fun otherwise. These kids are agile and flexible. They can yank off branches to help make base camps. They can jump across rocks without slipping. There is a lot of shouting, laughing and the usual jostling that young kids do.

Young Luke's grandmother regularly takes him for walks through the Kurnell bush to teach him about nature and culture and to teach him about connection to place. But playing with his cousins, learning to share resources equitably, understanding how to run and toss cones, dodge and laugh – that was something too. As Luke tells me now, 25 years later, he and his cousins learned from one another and gained a sense of place through the games that they played at Kurnell when he was a kid. It was a site of cultural learning in multiple ways.

When Luke tells me this childhood memory, the vivid joy of those moments is also an expression of Indigenous knowledges. Knowledge for Luke is about embedding memory into place and things. So, his realisation about playing with banksia cones and charging around the bush and redistributing resources is: 'Oh, I'm doing it, I'm doing culture.'

Now Luke is in his mid-thirties. He still has curly dark hair and has a matching beard. He is a highly respected poet. He has kind eyes and often wrinkles his forehead in thought. Part of my herbarium project is to ask poets to respond to specimens in the herbarium collection. Our team wanted to gauge how poets might interpret and revalue the specimens. I was curious how the creative process might represent the complexity of plants, or even their cultural and social history and meaning.

Luke Patterson is a Gamileroi man who lives and works on Gadigal land. He is Juncture Fellow with the *Sydney Review of Books* and a member of the 2022 Emerging Writers' Festival advisory board. He studied music, then linguistics, at Melbourne University. As part of the Charlie Perkins Aurora

Foundation program, he went on to the prestigious Berkeley University near San Francisco, where he studied folklore.

He explains that his folkloric work at Berkeley started as riddles, songs and myths in first year and then progressed to decolonial interpretations of folklore as evil. For Luke, decolonising is about the act of disenchanting and re-enchanting. He says, 'I think if you let it help you see how enchanted, for better or worse, your own cultural positions are, it can also help you find your own absurdity.'

In between writing his poems, he works with Aunty Barb Nicholson and her Dreaming Inside project, which involves teaching creative writing to Aboriginal and Torres Strait Islander inmates at the Junee correctional facility. So he is a very busy poet, and highly sought after.

When Amanda Lucas-Frith, editor of *Plumwood Mountain Journal*, and I commissioned Luke to write a poem for our project, he chose Old Man Banksia. Now that I have had a long chat with him about his poem, I understand why. When he was in primary school, Kurnell was 'absolutely saturated in colonial folklore which was such a bizarre cognitive dissonance'. Luke is talking about the giant replica anchors in the suburb and how his school's motto was *We endeavour* and his school houses were called Banks, Cook and Solander.

The colonial experience was embedded in Luke's childhood, despite his family's heritage and politics. Early in his primary school years, the best class for that month would be given the privilege of taking turns to bring home a special doll – a kind of school mascot – as a prize of sorts. I remember my own sons having this tradition at their primary school – theirs was a stuffed sheep. But the special prize at Luke's school was a four-foot-high (1.2-metre) Captain Cook doll that sat in a special chair. Luke says that when it was his turn to take it home, the look on his grandmother's face was quite something.

It wasn't until Luke got to university and started reading Cook's diaries that he first saw the weirdness of Kurnell's colonial folklore. He came to understand that the mythology around colonial heroes like Cook and Banks conceals the true history of violent British colonialism and even becomes a kind of trickery, because everyone believes the myths. He says, 'The myth of Banks is literally right in front of our faces, a history encoded into the name and language. But at the very same time, why is it hidden? Why is that meaning hidden? It seems utterly bizarre and it seems like a bad magic.'

Luke chose the banksia because, 'The name, the place that I grew up, there's a sympathetic relation of absence and unknowing despite something being right in your freaking face. I think also, of course, there's a particular more widespread relationship to folklore and banksia men and the racialisation of the plants in that way and the innocent fair little gumnut children. Along with the mythology and coloniality, the banksia made me feel the joy of childhood memories … when my cousins and I could have banksia wars and were just pelting these things at each other.'

I want to know what poetry means to Luke and whether it's a good way to connect with the herbarium plants. By way of answer, Luke says that poetry is not just describing something, but enacting it in some shape or form. He thinks people don't know whether poetry is fact or fiction. The rules are different and there are more possibilities.

Luke's poetry based on the banksia specimen has reminded me of how much colonial folklore is endemic in our everyday lives in Australia. Those white coloniser histories are so embedded, we barely notice they are there. Luke's work with the banksia, and his kindness in sharing his experience by writing about it, is exactly the re-enchantment he hopes for. I'll never look at a banksia cone again without remembering his story about his war games as a kid.

JOSEPH BANKS IN THE HERBARIUM

As you might expect, given Luke's observations about the banksia, there is controversy over its name. *Banksia serrata* or *B. serrata* is one of Australia's most-loved plants. It is found in sandy aeolian soils along the eastern coast of Australia, and can grow to become twisted and gnarled, with leathery rough bark. This tree travelled around the globe as early as 1770 to take up residence in habitats such as the Temperate House, a Victorian glasshouse at the Royal Botanic Gardens, Kew.

A very special *Banksia integrifolia* specimen sheet is located in the herbarium in Sydney, which I was lucky enough to see. It is kept in a secure freezer room where all the valuable Joseph Banks and Daniel Solander collections are stored. Banks (1743–1820) and Solander (1733–1782) are known as the dazzling duo of Australian botanical history.

Both were famous naturalists and explorers, and during April and May 1770 they spent five weeks at Kamay (Botany Bay) collecting plants as part of Captain Cook's expedition – an expedition that had such profound implications for the future of First Nations peoples. It isn't surprising that one of Australia's most identifiable plants was given the name banksia by Europeans, to commemorate the work of one of the most famous naturalists of his time. There are no notations of Aboriginal names on the specimen sheets for the same plant.

The day I was shown into the special freezer room, I took a photo on my phone of the banksia type. A type is like a first edition book, the master file. It is the specimen used the first time a plant is named and the specimen labelled. The freezer room where this banksia specimen is kept has a security box outside that requires a code and a hugely heavy fire-resistant external door.

Not everyone at the herbarium has access to this room. It is quite small, only about three metres by four metres, with a few specimen cupboards and some small freezers. The walls are white and the cupboards are white. The light is white and the whole experience in that room is a bit sci-fi. We were allowed to be there, but it was clearly where all the good stuff was kept and I was on my best behaviour and careful not to drop anything or knock anything or tear anything. I now keep my photo of this rare banksia on my computer and sometimes keep it open on my desktop because it is a powerful piece of history. To publish my photograph of it in an article or book, I must formally request permission, because it is a type. It is the specimen that bears the first-ever banksia name.

As Luke has pointed out, there is more than one side to the story of Joseph Banks in Australia's history, but in his time Banks was a revered botanist in England, and many landmarks in Australia still bear his name. He took 30 000 specimens from Australia and elsewhere to Kew Gardens for their collection. As recently as July 2022, a sculptural installation was built inside Lincoln Cathedral in northern England to commemorate his work.

American painter Benjamin West's 1773 portrait of Joseph Banks surrounded by objects from his collection is well known, and has been re-interpreted by Aboriginal artist Daniel Boyd with Banks depicted as a pirate. But back in 1773, not only were curious objects collected by travelling naturalists and botanists, but also the process of collecting was admired as part of the British imperial project. Collectors such as Banks were lauded; their careers were forged with these pilfered objects, which extended beyond the botanical. When the Bidjigal warrior Pemulwuy (1750?–1802), known for resisting the aggressions of colonial settlers, was shot dead, his head was cut off and sent to Joseph Banks.

So there are parallel stories of collecting and honouring, of exploitation and violence, that emanate from specimens like the banksia. You only have to read the original *Voyages of Discovery* by Captain Cook to pick up the condescending tone of the narrative, the descriptions of First Nations peoples as 'barbaric and uncivilised'.

There is a section where Cook describes Mr Banks and Dr Solander landing at a place called Otaheite (later renamed Tahiti) where 'hundreds of natives' came up to them and presented them with branches of trees as 'symbols of peace'.[3] The descriptions of the dwellings and activities of the 'natives' are filled with disdain. Twenty years later Banks would commission Captain William Bligh to take thousands of breadfruit plants from Otaheite on his ship *Providence* to Jamaica to cheaply feed the plantations' enslaved workers. This casing of Tahiti for economic gain is not mentioned in Cook's journals.

Many researchers and botanists now know that Banks was both a great botanist and an imperialist who pillaged the Pacific for the benefit of his collections and the glory of the British Empire. Yet still the naming of the banksia remains.

The famous plant classification expert Karl Linnaeus (1741–1783) published the banksia type name as *Banksia integrifolia* in 1782 to honour Joseph Banks.

Most taxonomists and botanists do not begrudge Banks this flattery, but it is mostly agreed that he was not someone concerned with preservation, or local acknowledgement, or conservation. To have such an iconic family of plants named after him sticks in many people's throats. That is the anguish that sits around decolonising Australia and particularly decolonising plants: it is not easy territory to navigate. As Luke says, for him, decolonising is a process of disenchanting and re-enchanting.

Despite its resilient beauty, for many Australians their perception of *B. serrata*'s seed cones is discoloured by the memory of the children's books by May Gibbs (1877–1969), who characterised the banksia cones as bad men who might steal your children. Bundjalung poet Evelyn Araluen has explored the rejection of Aboriginal bodies in Gibbs' *Snugglepot and Cuddlepie* and draws attention to her 'casting-out of the recurring villains, the Banksia Men, who are aligned with savagery, animism, sexual deviancy, and Aboriginality throughout the stories'.[4]

This absence of direct references to Aboriginal and Torres Strait Islander peoples (and the parallel racist analogies) is a reminder of Australia's history of massacres, genocides and stolen generations of Aboriginal children. This Australian experience mirrors other colonies around the world where Indigenous erasure takes many forms – not just from stories or archives, but via loss of land, pollution, and renaming of the landscape, all of which have lasting impacts not only socially but environmentally.[5]

As Māori scholar Linda Tuhiwai Smith says, 'Renaming

the land was probably as powerful ideologically as changing the land ...'[6] Absence and non-naming are as powerful politically as renaming.[7] If non-naming and renaming carry political and social weight, then including Aboriginal names in Western botanical classifications may be a complex but necessary process.

The naming of plants is important for worldwide knowledge about which plants grow where and how habitats change and how climate and weather changes are affecting plant growth. Sharon Willoughby is an environmental historian working at Kew Gardens in London with a background in ecological science. She has been extremely generous with her knowledge about the complexities of acknowledging Australian Aboriginal names.

She has noted that the *Atlas of Living Australia* website records only one Indigenous name for the banksia plant: *wiriyagan,* from the Cadigal people of the Sydney region of New South Wales.[8] Given that the natural distribution of *B. serrata* covers much of the eastern seaboard of Australia, passing though the nations and languages of many Aboriginal peoples, she believes it is likely that there are many more rich names for *B. serrata* that reflect subtleties in culture, season and situation.[9]

Naming is critical for ongoing production and sharing of botanical and ecological knowledge. It is also vital for conservation, for charting environmental changes and for adding new knowledge, which is crucial at this time of catastrophic climate and biodiversity crisis. Naming in European cultures also carries legacies of class, power, imperial dominance and coloniser exclusivity.

So decolonising plants might be a process of first uncovering the privilege and knowledge limitations of being white (European/Western) in Australia, of ensuring equal access to the full stories for all Australians, of ensuring ethical inclusion and Indigenous expertise and agency in those stories, and of better understanding the problems of lost languages and erased cultures.

Better understanding the banksia is probably a good start.

TWO-WAY BOTANY

I used to give my writing students the task of describing a tree – its trunk, bark, branches, roots, leaves, flowers, seeds – without naming the tree as a tree. The test was to describe the parts, without ever mentioning the whole. It can be harder for non-Indigenous people to do this than you might think. People who have grown up with a European heritage and education have a tendency to picture the whole natural object and to name it.

For many of us, it's hard not to think in a linear way, not to order chronologically, not to name in hierarchical patterns. For First Nations peoples, this seems to be less of a hindrance, with knowledge incorporating … well, incorporating everything. Sky, ocean, earth, stars, deep time, rocks, all kinship beings and the relationality of all beings and things.

When I asked the botanists and horticulturists I was starting to meet through the herbarium how that kind of thinking worked in terms of plants, a few people mentioned Gerry Turpin. 'The man who bridges two cultures,' they said. The plant guy who knows about traditional plant knowledge and Western knowledge too. Gerry Turpin is the first government-employed Indigenous ethnobotanist and runs the Tropical Indigenous Ethnobotany Centre in Cairns. He is a Mbabaram man from Country up near Atherton in Queensland.

Gerry has a plant named after him, the *Tephrosia turpinii*. He was able to help his colleague find specimens of the legume in difficult locations, and the colleague consequently named the plant in Gerry's honour. This name sits within the Western Linnaean taxonomic system. Gerry says, '*Tephrosia turpinii* is a legume. So, it flowers and it's a cultural plant as well. So that was the main reason they named it after me, it's the cultural plant for our community and Mbabaram nation. They [Traditional Owners] basically used the plant as a wash for skin, this is the plant I'm researching.'

Gerry is the first person to really explain 'Murri time' to me. I'd heard the term before and thought it referred to how Indigenous concepts of multiple time are different to Western versions of time that are more linear. But Gerry gives me an example of how, when he goes out to sit with Elders and they have yarning sessions round the fire to get to know each other better, there might be a moment that he thinks is the end. But then someone new starts talking. So 'Murri time' is not nine to five, it's any time of the day or night.

I talk with Gerry about it being time to address the most respectful way to name Australian plants. While the herbarium reflects the Western Linnaean system of taxonomic naming, there is an absence of Aboriginal names.

'But there has been lately a push to name new species after the Aboriginal name or the Aboriginal community,' Gerry replies. 'So, for example, the stinging jellyfish up here is Irukandji. So, that's the Irukandji nation, named after the Irukandji nation, and there's plants named after Aboriginal names as well. Not that many, but yeah, there is a bit of a push to name plants after Aboriginal names and even after Aboriginal people. It's important to consult with the community as they may not want traditional names or people's names used for various reasons.'

I'm still not sure what the naming similarities and differences are between Western and Indigenous naming. Gerry says that Aboriginal and Torres Strait Islander peoples 'do name plants' and 'they name parts of plants and sometimes the plant is just named after the action of the plants. So, I think the birds are named after the calls in most cases. So the name of the bird *is* the call, kind of thing. So there's various ways and all communities have different ways of naming their plants. Indigenous knowledge or Indigenous science is completely different.

'As you probably found out through your research, Indigenous knowledge is more holistic, so there's a connection to everything. So when I talk about plants, there's spiritual things. There's taboo things. There's lore. It's an indicator of something else [that] is happening on Country. So everything's just connected. Whereas Western science kind of zeros in on certain parts and there's just no way that you can bring the two together. And that's my interest, Indigenous biocultural knowledge working alongside Western science.'

Gerry works with his Mbabaram community to make decisions about certain plants, including protecting knowledge about traditional plants. When he first started working in this community, he didn't just go to mob with an idea of what he thought they were going to do. Instead he held workshops with leaders in the communities and other people interested in ethnobotany and asked them what they wanted.

'They came up and they just said, "First, we'd like to have our knowledge recorded." Because the Elders are getting on and they're passing on. And the kids, they move away from Country for various reasons. And they just wanted to document it and [have it] stored in a safe place so that the younger generations can come back later and still access that knowledge. So, that's the main reason why I do it, just to save the knowledge that is left for communities.'

Gerry records and documents traditional plant use up on the Cape York Peninsula, which includes setting up protocols and making sure they are followed. He was director of Indigenous engagement with the Ecological Society of Australia, with whom he started a Reconciliation Action Plan, which included protection of Indigenous cultural and intellectual property rights and Indigenous regeneration plans.

This means following an approach to botany called two-way. This is Indigenous and Western science working together. An example of two-way knowledge is fire management practice, which is used widely across Australia, especially since the 2019–2020 bushfires.

But Gerry says that 'some people think it's easier for me because I'm Aboriginal, but sometimes it's harder because they say that I should know about protocols and engagement. Whereas they expect white people to make mistakes, so sometimes it's harder. And for me it's still about that relationship-building first. So getting to know mob, learning from them and letting them get to know me before the project even starts. That's a matter of just yarning around the campfires, things like that. And even then, it takes a while to build trust.'

Experts such as Gerry are unsurprisingly cautious when it comes to plants and plant use, especially medicinal or cultural plant use. This is because in the past, pharmaceutical companies have taken plants like eucalyptus and made multimillion-dollar profits without acknowledging or remunerating cultural knowledge owners. Although Queensland has the *Biodiscovery Act*, there are still vulnerabilities regarding patenting of native plants for profit.

There are community laws, lore and languages that need to be learned and understood, Gerry explains. 'Some plants have lores attached to them or taboos. For example, certain plants should not be consumed until a male is initiated. Some plants are viewed as Ancestors or have value in other areas. These complex involvements are often overlooked by Western scientists who tend to study just the physical aspects of the plant rather than its spiritual or cultural relationships.'[10]

While this information is fascinating, Gerry reminds me of the negative truth: his people have lost a lot of culture. 'Mbabaram people, my mob, we've only got about 300 words left in the language. And when the miners came in and the farmers, our people were either chased off or massacred or shifted to missions. And that's when that connection to Country was cut and connection to culture and language.'

An artist colleague of mine was given the totem of the koala by her family, and I ask Gerry if he has a totem animal or tree. He said that for the Mbabaram language group, the totem is the emu. But for their clan group, they've just chosen the dove. 'It's there,' he says. 'The native dove, which has an Aboriginal name of *gulidin*.'

Is there a special tree for him?

He tells me he connects to the peanut tree, because it's a multiple-use tree – it's edible, and it's medicinal as well. The bark can also be useful for making twine for dilly bags or fishing nets.

'The peanut tree is just a big shady tree and I just like it,' he says. 'I'll probably do more research on it, on the medicinal side. That's the thing. Culture is not static. It's dynamic. And the Elders always say, when you go into Country, the Country will teach you things. So, that's how you can build up your culture and customs again, you can start from scratch.'

ZOMBIE FUNGUS AND THE BLACK DRINK

Zombies are in-between species.[11] They are the living dead, the halfway point between the two states but not quite either. As bewitched corpses, zombies don't feel or understand or empathise. I mean, so we imagine. In a way, the specimen sheets in the herbarium are in-between zombie objects too. They are real biotic life but they are kept in an inert, even deadened, way.

In popular culture zombies are associated with malevolent, purposeful infection. They stagger around in movies catastrophically infecting everyone, as though there is no one left to trust. This could be a reflection of our times, or it could be a peripheral comment on survivalist theories regarding all ecological cycles.

Either way, Miguel Garcia knows about zombies. He is a living encyclopedia, which is not surprising, given he's a librarian. He is the librarian of the Daniel Solander Library at the Royal Botanic Garden, Sydney. When I chatted to Miguel, he was in the process of moving part of the library out to the new herbarium digs at Mount Annan, but the main part of the library would stay at the Domain.

The books he is taking out to the new herbarium, about 100 taxonomic books, will work just like the original herbarium library, in that the books that relate to each section of plant families will be stored next to those specimen sheets for easy access. This is knowledge integrated into the collection. The rest of the library includes journals, botanical illustrations and archaeological material such as colonial ceramics, old bottles, Dutch clay pipes from early colonisers – but nothing Indigenous. The archaeological material the library holds was unearthed from the Domain many years after the great fire of 1882 that destroyed the Garden Palace.

The Garden Palace was constructed on a hill in the Domain overlooking Sydney harbour for the 1879 International Exhibition. It had a huge glass dome and was designed in the mould of London's Crystal Palace – a monument to imperial collecting that exhibited cultural objects, such as an 1878 Bechstein grand piano. However, three years later, a dawn fire engulfed the mostly wooden structure, destroying almost everything within and creating a fiery red scene on the hill. Nearly a thousand Aboriginal and Torres Strait Islander artefacts were burned.

Miguel is interested in the history of botany, which he believes is connected to medicine. In 2015 he curated an exhibition called 'Herbals: Myth, Magic and Medicine'. In this exhibition he explored plant medicine that could be ingested, brewed as tea, drunk as a tincture or breathed in. Miguel is aware of the Australian and international discourse on psychoactive plants and notes that it arose out of plants' usefulness for our health.

'Cultures around the world,' he explains, 'revolved around plant culture and that relationship was part of South American or South Pacific rituals and belief systems and societies.' He is thinking about peyote or the black drink made of native holly plants often added to emetic (vomit-inducing) herbs, a ritualistic beverage meant to purify and cleanse. Australians who have visited Fiji on holiday may have heard of kava or yaqona, a traditional communal drink shared by Fijians for its narcotic and sedative effects.

The black drink was popular across Native American lands north of Mexico during pre-Columbian times. There is evidence that the holly leaves created a highly caffeinated drink that was drunk as black tea before war, before ceremonies, before political meetings.[12] The object was to purify those partaking of it by vomiting.

The Solander library has various parts that include ethnobotany (cultural use and perception) and medical botany (medical science and botany). The books and illustration plates date back to the 1490s. Aboriginal ethnobotany has not been well-documented but there is work being done by researchers, including Indigenous researchers such as Gerry Turpin at the Cairns herbarium, working with communities to redress this.

There are issues of trust with this kind of work, including issues around appropriate sharing of knowledge and previous unscrupulous commercial exploitation of such knowledge. Arguably this work should be undertaken by Indigenous-led projects rather than via the paternalistic approaches of most white institutions and university methodologies, which can be extractive.

As Miguel explains, 'The physic gardens preceded the botanic gardens, and ethnobotany became modern medicine. So herbal knowledge, often stored within the lives of women, is an important precursor to contemporary disease prevention and treatment. In the library collections are books, plates and specimens that illustrated human health. The library collection is a lens upon the history of society. For instance, there is a photo in the archive of a 50-foot [15-metre] stand of cannabis plants in the Royal Botanic Garden's medicinal garden. A huge swing against psychoactive medicinal plants happened in the 1970s.' Miguel says this was due to a spate of deaths from people ingesting mushrooms for a psychoactive experience. 'Many native Australian mushrooms look alike and many are also poisonous. In fact, many herbal plants are extremely dangerous.'

Miguel's favourite plant is not a plant but is in the spirit collection room. It is an ophio-cordycep. A zombie fungus! He says there are many different species of genus that attack insects such as grubs or caterpillars. His favourite is a witchetty grub in a collection jar that has fungus growing out of its head.

So the fungus sends out its mycelial threads and those little fungi eventually take control of innocent insects. They take over the insect's nervous system and brain. Then the witchetty grub, in this instance, is compelled to act by the fungus. So the grub burrows through the soil and when it gets up to the surface, the fruiting body of the fungus pops out of the ground and bursts out its spores. Interestingly, Miguel also tells me that in some cultures, such as in south-east Asia, the whole infected grub with its infecting fungus is highly sought after. They are made into tea or tonics and sell for $14 000 per kilogram.

'Eight per cent of Nepal's GNP is the export of these dried fungi because it has mild psychoactive and aphrodisiac effects, intended for general good health and wellbeing,' Miguel says. 'Even back in the fifth century BCE in China, people used this zombie fungus.'

Zombie fungus, then, is the legacy of ethnomycology (the relations between people, plants and mushrooms) that still exists today. Ethnobotany is the interaction of humans with plants, not just for food and shelter but also as medicine of all types. This specimen was obviously too big and ugly to mount on a paper specimen page, so it sits among the many other plants in jars in the spirit collection room at the herbarium, although it really should be in a fungarium.

All the specimens in this room look like alien creatures or mutated examples of horrifying nature gone wrong. No wonder the ghoulish among us love the herbarium so much.

THE UGLY HORNWORT

A small herbarium plant caught my eye. Well, when I say a plant caught my eye, it was really the disintegrating remnant of a plant that grabbed my attention. A hornwort. An ugly little hornwort's corpse. It is these kinds of plants that remind me that creative acts can make sense of non-human things – seeing this little plant made me think of witchcraft and herbalism, but first let me introduce it to you.

In its natural habitat, the hornwort is a fernlike, mossy, vibrantly green plant that thrives in aquatic environs. In death, on the specimen sheet, this hornwort is a dusty pile of undistinguished matter. A small dark mound of rich decomposed plant life – perhaps one gram's worth. When I first laid eyes on it, I confess I thought it would make good compost.

The hornwort is a non-vascular plant that spreads across woodland floors or attaches to rocks or trees and is known as a coloniser of other plants' habitats. A bryophyte. Bryophytes are the oldest land plants on our planet, as old as 400 million years. Hornworts are small, often measuring only a few centimetres or smaller. This little specimen in the herbarium, *Ceratophyllum demersum*, is not one little hornwort but a cluster of tiny hornwort plants.

'Held' is an interesting term to use for the individual entities in an archival collection. The herbarium is a major institution with a major 'holding' of multiple plants both native and otherwise from Australia and across the world. Holding? Held hostage? Held against one's will? Or held as in embraced? Or held as in cupped carefully in the palm of one's hand?

The herbarium cares for the specimens it holds. There are the two sets of security doors, the climate control – of both moisture and temperature – and there is the constant care to avoid the worst danger to a collection archive of 1.4 million specimens. By which I mean the tiny insects that can infest and decimate an entire collection of national significance.

So the 'holding' has multiple meanings whereby we can understand that the herbarium takes care of its guests but also contains a history of cultural neo-colonialism and nation-building – the collecting of rare objects for the pleasure of a dominant first-world country. This can be the collecting of rare and precious specimens from places that may not give permission or where permission had not been obtained. These are activities that underscore imperial power or dominion over nature or one country's supremacy over another, and have caused harm, for instance to Indigenous peoples. At what cost were some of these specimens collected? What is the difference between taking a biotic object without permission, and stealing?

Who among us is the real plant thief?

When I saw it, this little pile of earthy hornwort matter sitting in its pristine white plastic tub had been removed from its paper envelope that had been removed from a manila folder that had been taken from a claret-red plastic collection box that had been taken from a shelf. It was moving along a black conveyor belt to be digitally photographed by a state-of-the-art camera, and it was a melancholy sight.

Photographing all these inert plant objects (the herbarium has been photographing its entire collection) that were once living sparks questions relating to representation and expression. Who will see these new images and how do they relate to the original archive specimen and its former life? But at the point of death (which in vegetal life is less obvious than vascular human life) there is a moment when the plant is still very beautiful. For instance the pressed flower, the bulbous seed in its specimen jar or the packet of seeds stapled next to the leaf specimen, are still at a point of decomposition.

The specimens in the herbarium are often not quite dead. This state of life–death flux carries romantic weight as it reminds us of human mortality. These specimens also continue in the form of a life of study – for plant physiology research, for medicinal and economic and cultural legacy and knowledge of life past, for botanical illustrations or reawakened Indigenous knowledges. For inter-herbaria exchange. These are the activities of the herbarium and so, for some time after they have ceased to grow in soil, these specimens continue to have a lively and endlessly energetic status.

But my little hornwort friend? No, not so much. It really was a sad-sack of a specimen.

Nevertheless, it was the very first specimen of the herbarium's 1.4 million to be digitally photographed. A photographic representation of an object exists independent of the object it depicts. It has a new life as part of a digital archive but also exhibits a trace of the original.

I wondered about the former life of the hornwort, and started to think of how plants change but also have been used to change human perception, such as early medicine and herbalism, otherwise known as witchcraft. Think of hemlock, bloodroot, anise, rosewater and yew twig as ingredients for potions for death, for protection, for love. Plants have been conventionally 'used' for food, agriculture, medicine, shade, weapons. Elixirs, potions, balms and tonics have been used in Western and Eastern communities, past and present alike. These kinds of superstitious or religious or spiritual oppositions are often present in some aspect of our lives. Superstitions and plant potions have a long history of making changes in human behaviour and our affective, biological and mental states.

Later that night, having met the hornwort and considered its herbalist past, I decided to write a spell for it. To honour it and to remember that witchcraft and spells were meant as cures and often involved the use of plants.

Spell for the Hornwort

Coolant of stings and comfort of swelling,
Green pendant swinging on a string of barbed envy,
These pages are too heavy to turn alone.
Help me find the spell to return to watery depths
Where friendly mosses and liverworts comfort in the change
Single-celled spores and swimming biflagellate,
Plants that moved from sea to shore
May return without ressentiment poison
Clutching at their roots.

Spells are not frivolous. They are sibling to the poem. They are an exchange, a cultural act, a writing ritual. Spells are a shift in perception of a plant's value and even a way of getting closer to plants. With the spell ringing in my ear, I researched this specimen. It was collected on 1 April 1889. *Anthoceros dichotomus raddi* is the title on the specimen paper sheet. The specimen is small – a clump measuring 3 by 5 centimetres. It is a duplicate specimen, which was sent to the New South Wales herbarium (at some point not documented) as an exchange.

It was collected by Carlo Pietro Stefano Sommier (1848–1922) from Isola Gorgona, Italy. There is no description of the natural habitat it was collected from, nor the details of the circumstances of the collecting. Isola Gorgona, west of Livorno, is the smallest island of the Tuscan Archipelago. It is a typical Italian island – soaring cliffs on one side that plunge down into the deep sea, and a pretty bay on the other side where a fishing village is nestled. There is purple heather and the rock face is dark stone, wildly dissimilar from the pinkish honey of our Sydney sandstone. However, in addition to the village, the island is home to a prison, which was established in 1861. Visitors to the island are severely regulated, with only 75 allowed each day.

Extant images of the island make it look like it is stuck in the 1950s. The buildings and concreted bayside have a distinctly retro look. Sommier collected his hornwort from this island in 1889, 28 years after the Grand Duke of Tuscany changed the island from being the site of a religious community of monks to being the site of a prison. Sommier, born and raised in Florence, started collecting in 1870, so he had almost 20 years of collecting experience by the time he grabbed this little clump.

For me, there is a romantic allure to the notion of exploring isolated islands and collecting specimens for an herbarium archive. This is exploratory work, conducted by scientists and amateur collectors alike. The late nineteenth century was a particularly active time for this kind of collecting.

A drive to possess and dominate, to succumb to the allure of acquiring things, can manifest in collecting plants for an institution. This plant-collecting craze was more than self-flattering nationhood or cultural status – it also revealed the value of rare plants that could be used for propagation and bought and sold in the marketplace.

So while there was a culture of swapping specimens among herbaria, there was also an economic game at play. For example, in 1850 the Scottish collector John Jeffrey, known for collecting mosses and hornworts, was despatched to North America by a group of wealthy British investors. Jeffrey soon realised many other plant collectors had already travelled through these lands. The archives in the Royal Botanic Garden in Edinburgh record Jeffrey's travels and details of his collections, including the latitude and longitude of the plants he found.[13]

In its medicinal use, the hornwort traditionally acts as a cooling agent for biliousness and scorpion stings. There have been studies of the medicinal properties of the hornwort. The Cancer Council conducted work in 1986 on the facility of the hornwort (and mosses and liverworts) to act as anti-tumour agents.[14] The study was interesting in that it was reviewed from various perspectives including folklore, chemo-therapeutic potential, taxonomy and active compounds. The study tested for biological activity and the ability of bryophytes to absorb toxins, rather than collating data on evidence of cures. This was a hypothesis of potentials.

A connection can be drawn between scientific studies such as the one conducted by the Cancer Council and the activities of the spell-casters. The witches' spells and protective incantations, the folkloric administering of plant cures and links to Western medicine all pivot on the importance of getting the dose right. The hornwort lacks true roots, but certain leaves function to help anchor the plant in the substrate. Spells may lack social status but the relevance of ritual, written and spoken, can anchor humans in the earth and remind us of everything we do not know.

And the humble hornwort? We know that the earth's first terrain plants evolved from the sea. We know that the hornwort has anti-inflammatory properties. We know that the little pile of sooty dirt in the collection of the National Herbarium of New South Wales was the first specimen in the collection to be digitised and is therefore the first object to be established as cultural legacy representing past human–plant relations that have now been lost. But … that's all I know.

'BARBARA IS AMAZING'

The field of botanical science and its speckled history is broad, deep and rich. Earthy. Its roots interact with other trees of interest and there is a connectedness that mimics the subjects of its study. There are several established 'old-school' botanists who have travelled through mainstream education and professional careers and can offer informed versions of the herbarium's history.

Without a doubt, every single person associated with the Royal Botanic Garden I talked to, who knows Barbara Briggs, softened when I mentioned her name. Barbara is revered by young botanists and by managing staff, by archivists, horticulturists, executive managers and collectors. She began working with the gardens as a young botanist in 1959, and went on to become head of science.

She named a buttercup (*Rununculus acrophilus*) that grows only up on the summit of Mount Kosciuszko, and many other plants, but is perhaps best known for her plant evolution work, which she saw develop from 1960 into the fast-paced DNA technology of the present day.

I met Barbara Briggs many months after I first heard of her. Her reputation made me a little more nervous than usual as I waited in the foyer of the offices of the Royal Botanic Garden in the Domain. It didn't help that an eastern koel was watching me from high in a eucalyptus tree as I arrived. Its dark eyes followed me until I disappeared inside, but its energy stayed with me.

She arrived, a neat figure, quietly spoken and exuding a calm confidence. Barbara showed me through the security doors and led me to a back corner of the library, where we found a couple of armchairs. Broken white sculptures lay incongruously on the carpet at our feet. The library was silent and we sat facing out through the floor-to-ceiling windows to the canopy of palms outside.

First, Barbara explained that it was her mother who introduced her to the world of science and encouraged her to pursue it. She regularly took Barbara on bushwalks and would point out things of interest such as sedimentary rock. Barbara's mother was the first woman in New South Wales to graduate with a physics degree and Barbara followed in her academic footsteps and completed her botanical taxonomy PhD at Sydney University in 1960.

As a girl, Barbara had become interested in various sciences – zoology, biology and geology – but she had to choose. Geology was her first love because of all the fossils and rock formations she had met in the Blue Mountains during her school holidays. But soon enough botany piqued her curiosity and she became interested in the evolutionary elements of plants – a thread that became the heart of her doctoral thesis and continued to motivate her through the course of her career. For her, botany and geology were connected because of how the tectonic movement of the continents affected plants.

In Australia, Gondwanic plants came back when the southern continents united. There is more plant dispersal across oceans than is realised from the original supercontinents, Barbara explains, and this can be seen in the crossovers between plants in Madagascar and other southern countries.

Barbara has worked with the proteaceae family of plants. Her hypothesis is that the history of the proteaceae family was aligned to the history of the geological shifting of the continents, combining her youthful interests in both geology and botany.

Barbara now believes we are in a golden age of biology because of the new precision of scientific technology. For Barbara, who used to visually count chromosomes, the capacity of technology to analyse DNA means that she has been able to better understand the phylogeny or family connections of plants.

An example of the biological evolution that Barbara is talking about is the story of the moths called 'black wings'. In nineteenth-century England, when there were record levels of soot and pollution in the air from industrialisation, the local moths changed the colour of their wings for protection.

Barbara has also done work on the restionaceae family, which are related to grasses, sedges or rushes. These grasses are perennials and their pollen gets blown around in the wind, which helps them pollinate.

'I thought I'd get to my unfinished projects when I retired,' she says. 'I see climate change as an urgent policy issue. Now we have DNA and computer science tools and even though it might seem like I've done minor corrections to family trees – which may not seem exciting – watching the new grad students doing new work in this area is very exciting.'

Geological time scales are hard to understand or predict but Barbara's legacy will be the work she did in the plant families proteaceae and restionaceae. This knowledge will stand the test of time. Even though much botanical and taxonomic work is mundane, it changes our thinking about more than plants, affecting entire ecologies of shifting circumstances and possibilities for renewal.

Barbara also has interesting things to say about women in botany. Rather than decrying the lack of acknowledgement of female botanists, she believes that women are strongly represented in the field.

'When I started in 1959, the gardens were attached to the Department of Agriculture. Shortly after that, I started as head of science. As part of that, we had team meetings as part of the Department of Agriculture and they were mostly meetings of men, but the men were polite.'

Barbara Briggs is 87 and she notes that her parents saw a huge amount of change but she believes she has seen even more. She says young students at the garden constantly surprise her and she tries to maintain that glimmer of excitement. In her career Barbara has named 80 plants.

'Conservation is achieved through naming and taking note,' she says. 'There is so much we don't know. What we don't know is an important part of the work. Better to have the basis of what is there first. And then what needs to be cared for.'

DISCOVERING THE MONSTER

I'm conflicted about the GLAM sector. GLAM is an acronym for galleries, libraries, archives and museums. These institutions are complicated places. They leave many of us torn between knowing that many collections were sourced unethically or at best insensitively, while loving the bounty and the rich stories of the objects they contain.

The John Sloane Museum in London is a perfect example. I visit it whenever I'm in London because it is eclectic and eccentric, generous and rich, showing paintings and natural history. It's a beautiful and romantic place of study with wood panels and winding back staircases and intimate library areas. Sloane was a collector of curios such as a rhino horn grown into a tree root or a mummy's finger. He collected remedies and curiosities like gloves knitted from the beards of many mussels. He studied both medicine and botany and used three different cataloguing systems and had an embossed mark for all works on paper.

But I also know that in 2020, the British Museum removed a bust of Sloane from their exhibition galleries because he was involved in slavery. Sloane married a wealthy heiress who owned sugar plantations worked by slaves in Barbados and Jamaica. He worked as a doctor on these plantations and tried to promote inoculation against smallpox. This may sound benign, but as Londa Schiebinger reveals in her 2017 book, *Secret Cures of Slaves*, during this period doctors performed terrible experiments on adults and children on these plantations in a race to cure the disease.

These are the confounding issues that hound collections, museums and ongoing collection processes and legacies. The herbarium and its staff have similar stories to tell.

I met Hannah McPherson, director of the herbarium, at its home in the Domain in early 2020. She led me through reception and into the DNA lab, which looks out onto a rocky garden of ferns. Hannah, like many other plant scientists, learned to extract DNA from plants and seeds as part of her work. We passed work benches, lab flasks, petri dishes and white coats hanging on pegs.

At last we arrived in the herbarium collection area. With its rows and rows of shelves and the endless grid of red boxes, the herbarium collection area smelled as an archive should ... slightly musty. (Not so good for the plants.) Dampness and insects are an herbarium manager's worst nightmare. Even though the gardens were not having dampness problems, there was that lingering stench of time: old paper, things not quite dried out, biotic matter in abiotic places.

Hannah led me up and down the corridors, pausing to open up plant specimen boxes. Page after page of specimens taped to sheets of the same size. Typed text and handwritten texts, seeds in bags attached to the sheets. She said that digitising and moving the collection was a very useful process because it was uncovering new treasures such as Margaret Flockton's illustrations and coloured specimen sheets that were dotted throughout the whole collection.

Margaret Flockton (1861–1953) was an Australian botanical illustrator who worked at the herbarium between 1901 and 1927 and contributed to several books on flora and eucalyptus produced by the Royal Botanic Garden. There are a thousand of Flockton's illustrations in the archive and many appear on the herbarium sheets. Hannah describes them as being, 'Like morse code. Like tagging. The signature of collectors and illustrators through history, across objects.'

Originally the plant archive was conflated with the library because it was all considered original source material. The herbarium plants and the library books kept each other company. For instance, the lichen specimen section had lichen books stacked at its end. Hannah led me to one huge tome, *Gerard's Herball*. It was heavy and had marbled endpapers. These books often started with medicinal herbs, the utility of the garden, the uses of plants. They were usually collated by barber-surgeons – barbers who, due to their skill with sharp blades, could turn from shaving and cutting hair to being battlefield surgeons amputating limbs.

There was an established company of barber-surgeons in England in the sixteenth and seventeenth centuries, and John Gerard was one of them. He had a passion for gardening and started the barber-surgeon physic garden in London. Barber-surgeons and their apprentices were often plucked from the military and 'could cut well'. Published in 1636, the copy of *Gerard's Herball* in the herbarium library dates from this era of the barber-surgeon and represents medicinal knowledge of that time.

It is no surprise that Hannah was leading me through elements of the collection, like a master narrator. Her background is in books. One of her first job titles was Assistant Conservator of the Sir Hans Sloane Collection of Vegetables and Vegetable Substances at the Natural History Museum London. She was at the Natural History Museum for one year in 2003 and spent six months as conservator and six months as lichen curator.

Hannah explained that she likes the herbarium collection, 'Because we can understand the collection now but also the dusty stories and the old information adds to the story. It's alive. They are valuable not because they are old, but [because] they have currency now. The herbarium collection is a current research collection.'

Hannah first researched the German botanical collector Amalie Dietrich (1821–91) when she got a 2009 scholarship to research and curate a project at the Herbarium Hamburgense on Amalie's botanical collections. Amalie's husband, Wilhelm, was a pharmacist who collected plants for pharmaceutical products and leaned on his wife, who already had skills in this field, to assist him.

However, when Wilhelm started an affair with their nanny, Amalie chose to leave her daughter Charitas and her now ex-husband in Germany to follow her collecting passion. She did not return for nearly a decade. In 1863 she was commissioned (after several years of trying) by the wealthy shipping merchant Johann Cesar VI Godeffroy to voyage from Hamburg to Australia to collect specimens for the newly established Museum Godeffroy.

Amalie faced harsh conditions and a heavy dose of misogyny as a female collector travelling alone during the late nineteenth century. Working mostly in remote regions of Queensland, she collected plants, rocks and animals, and must have been a woman of substantial character, if not indefatigable obsession. Her enviable and rigorous collections were widely respected and had an enormous impact on zoological and botanical knowledge for many decades to come.

She was able, despite the enormous physical and cultural challenges she faced in Australia, to constantly ship the specimens back to Hamburg for the Godeffroy Museum.

As Hannah explains, the collection was later moved to the National Museum of Hamburg, the ethnographic collection to Leipzig and the plants to the Hamburg Herbarium. In World War II the collections were moved again and only rediscovered in the 1980s.

As Hannah worked with the Godeffroy collection in 2009 she earmarked duplicates to send back to Australia for botanists to look at. The Sydney herbarium has 368 duplicates of Amalie's collection. Hannah says, 'Specimens become the truth.' She looked through Amalie's writings and found dates and places of collecting: 'If we have her full collection, then we can verify where and when she was whilst in Australia.' As it turned out, Hannah was right. Specimens do become the truth. They can reveal some unpleasant truths about their collectors.

Hannah explained the immense reputation that Amalie earned: '[Her collections] constitute the first records of many Australian species and provide a unique record of the Australian flora prior to land-clearing for expanding agriculture and urbanisation. Dietrich's immense contribution to natural history was recognised by her peers and successors, and many species are named in her honour.' Hannah also noted that much of Amalie's collections has still not been catalogued.

Hannah showed me a photograph of Amalie Dietrich. In it, she has clear round eyes, her thin lips pressed together in a calm expression. It was Amalie's mother who taught her about the wild plants and their medicinal uses as a child growing up in Saxony.

The Amalie I saw in Hannah's photo looks like she was capable of anything and in effect she was. A long sea voyage, and a brutal life on the backroads of Queensland would not have been easy for anyone, let alone a woman on her own.

Over those nine years, Amalie amassed what was then the most significant spider collection in the world, along with collections of marsupials, beetles, butterflies, coral, sea slugs and 20 000 plant specimens.

It turns out that each of Amalie's plant collections contained at least one specimen for the Museum Godeffroy and in most cases several duplicate specimens. The specimens were to be displayed in the museum in sets and duplicate sets were to be sold to raise revenue for the museum. In October 1866 a catalogue entitled *Plants of New Holland collected by Mrs. Amalie Dietrich at the Brisbane river, Col., Queensland by order of Mr Joh. Ces. Godeffroy & Son in Hamburg* was issued. It contained a list of almost 350 plant species available for purchase in sets. Amalie also collected ethnological specimens such as Aborignal canoes, clubs and spears. She collected 266 species of birds.

Hannah said that while Amalie was in Rockhampton, she collected one of her most important specimens, a brown snake that was new to Western science at the time and would later be commonly known as the taipan. Hannah said, 'Amalie Dietrich's collections were immensely important in Europe at a time when little was known about Australian flora and fauna.'

The collections remain as evidence of a unique period in the expansion of the natural sciences and global exploration by other German botanists – a rich history that included German botanist Ferdinand von Mueller (1825–96) and German naturalist and explorer Ludwig Leichhardt (1813–48), who went missing in the Australian landscape. Aside from their cultural and historical value, the specimens collected by Amalie Dietrich also remain important to the scientific community. However, there was more to the story of Amalie

Dietrich than being a key figure in the expansion of German botanical knowledge.

This was a period when women were not considered capable or equal to their male counterparts. Amalie would have been on the receiving end of discrimination and sexism. It is possible that she was not accepted into Australian squattocracy society (such as it was up round Rockhampton and Bowen). Even in the late 1970s and early 1980s, I remember the strict divisions between men and women working on the land in rural New South Wales. Women were still mostly expected to make the food while the men were out mustering the cattle. This was more than a function of physical capacity or strength, ability or experience. It was also about the pressure on women to be feminine and homely, to create nurturing domestic environments. My memories are of men smoking rollies, stamping their boots and spitting.

Back in the 1860s, for Amalie to have collected all that plant and fauna and ethnographic material from remote places such as Lake Elphinstone, she must have been strong. In nature, in spirit and physically. But perhaps she needed to be something else. It was an era of imperial expansion, and Britain was not alone in this: there were Dutch, French and German explorers in Australia who were also combing the land for interesting and curious objects.

As French philosopher Jacques Derrida said, monsters cannot be announced. Amalie's *volkerkunde* (anthropology) was as substantial as her botany. In the late 1860s she collected some specimens that most of us would find gruesome, if not unethical. From the Bowen area, she collected the skeletons of eight Aboriginal persons, five male and three female, plus a skull from Rockhampton.

I know Amalie was working at a time of biological determinism but it's hard to stomach. Darwin had just published *On the Origin of Species* in 1859. Scientists around the world were exploring theories of racial superiority and the measurement of skulls (comparative craniology) was part of this investigation about allegedly different cognitive abilities. The European view was that this was legitimate scientific procedure.

However, researcher Ray Sumner adds an extra layer of horror to Amalie's story by referring to a letter written by one of the Archers, a Rockhampton family, who lived at a property called Gracemere. According to Archer's letter, Amalie stayed with them and asked if one of their employees could shoot 'an Aborigine' so she could have his 'skeleton and pelt' as a specimen.[15]

We will never know how Amalie came to send eight full skeletons and one skull back to Germany. There are fragments of evidence that they were most likely stolen from burial places. It's hard not to consider the brutal and disrespectful details of such an activity.

Once you hear this story, you cannot unhear it. However, the only way to banish the real monsters is to face up to what they have done. It's true that Amalie's plant collections have been, and still are, critical for our understanding of local habitats and plant varieties prior to colonial agriculture and land-clearing. Many of her specimens are not mounted but are still physically wrapped up in the local newspapers from Brisbane. So, the specimens tell a social and cultural story as well as a scientific story.

As I walked away that day, I felt the lingering horror of Amalie's story, and it made my legs tremble. I touched the euphorbias and correas for comfort as I wound my way back to my car. I stopped in lower Woolloomooloo and reached out to touch one of the eucalypts to settle my mood. But the truth of Amalie's story still hasn't left me.

UNCLE IVAN

Eucalyptus leaves crackle dryly in summer but in winter, as the greener leaves slide against one another on the branch, they sound different notes, more like a violin bow. When people tell you that plants are talking to them, it makes sense, because every movement, when leaves rub together and branches squeak or groan, strikes different chords. There are also the sounds of water moving inside the trunk and the scuttling of ants on bark and wasps on gumnut flowers. Don't forget the movement of mycelium underneath the soil. If you care to listen.

There is a lot of scepticism about the capacity of plants to communicate. Putting aside the new discoveries of plant science around behaviours such as consciousness and intelligence, decision-making and memory, there is a long history of debate around plant communication.[16] We now know that plants communicate information via emitting hormones and gases (volatile chemicals). This information relates to nutrients and water supply via their root systems through complex webs of mycelium. We also anecdotally know that plants seem to grow stronger and better if we talk to them or play music to them. Though this latter provocation has not been proven.

Having said that, I know that trees talk to me. I hear what they say, when the wind moves their leaves and rustles their needles. I know what they say because it's always the same bloody thing they say to me. Over and over. No matter how many questions I ask the trees, they still give me the same answer.

I've tried to get a different message from different trees.

I've tried to hear a different tale from trees in different locations, but there is only one thing the trees say to me. 'Just don't worry so much', they say. Obviously I don't pay enough heed to the trees; if I did, they might give me a new message.

There is a huddle of casuarinas behind the row of houses that faces my house. Sometimes, I'll be at my front door and hear them roar over to me.

My whole body hears the casuarina message when it comes. I can feel my fingers tingle and my shoulders relax. My jaw slackens to a more gentle position and I find my whole body turning upwards to the trees. *Stop worrying*, they dully roar. And I do, for a while, and I smile as well. My daughter can tell when I'm listening to the casuarina trees. She'll be lugging her school bag just behind me, stop, see my face and say, 'You're listening to the trees again, aren't you?'

Yep, I am. And I'm grateful.

*

Stories come in different forms. The day I meet Uncle Ivan Wellington for lunch, his shoes are too tight. Uncle Ivan, a Yuin man, is one of the Elders of the Camden and Campbelltown area. He is the man the herbarium staff turn to for information about plant knowledge and expert advice on cultural care. I am here to meet Uncle Ivan on the first day of sunshine after 17 days of rain and floods in 2022. There, just outside the Campbelltown Art Centre, Uncle Ivan is wrestling to free his feet from shoes that are, as he explains, tightening as he wears them, rather than loosening up.

Uncle Ivan gives me an open grin and invites me to wait for him down in the café while he sorts out his shoes. Soon enough we are sitting at a sunny outdoor table and reflecting on the horrendous deluge that has flooded the Northern

Rivers. Here in Sydney, the local birds are busy with their songs and the sun is hitting the back of my left arm just enough to warm me but not to burn. Uncle Ivan leans back and takes a deep calm breath. I have my notepad and pen lined up on one side, and I have my phone, neat and ready, on the other side. Poised for recording, as always. On the notepad is my list of questions.

Uncle Ivan has a round, open face. He's 75 years old and listens with all of his direct attention. It occurs to me that this is a lost art: to listen, 100 per cent, to the person speaking. It inspires a matching response. So, before I press 'record' on my phone, I start to listen.

Uncle Ivan grew up in Kiama and the Nowra–Shoalhaven area. He'd roam the sandhills with his family and friends and eat pigface if he was hungry. Pigface is a succulent plant that grows across the dunes and is now a delicacy that sometimes appears on expensive restaurant menus.

'The place I grew up was Roseby Park, that's the white word for it. But my land is Jerrinja. That's called the place of the winds.' he says. There is something about the way he speaks that sounds … like the wind. A breath. Breathe in and breathe out. The wind can gently pull branches, tousle your hair and tug at your clothes. But sometimes it can yank, and break and rip.

Uncle Ivan grew up under the Aboriginal Protection Board. These boards were set up around Australia in the nineteenth century and controlled Aboriginal people's rights – where they lived, where they could travel, even who they could marry. In 1940 the *Aboriginal Welfare Act* proposed that Aboriginal peoples under the protection of the boards should be assimilated into mainstream society. The board was abolished in 1969.

Uncle Ivan stretches back as a waitress arrives for our order. Straight up, he strikes up a chat with the young girl and makes her so at ease that she asks if she can ask him a question. He holds out his arms in an open gesture: yes. What should she call the time before white colonisation and what should she should call it now, she asks. Ivan nods slowly and replies that his great-great-great-grandpa was an old leader by the name of Bundle who knew the Macarthurs (white colonisers who were the landed gentry of the Camden area).[17] Bundle belonged to the Wollemiri tribe.

Uncle Ivan tells the girl, 'White people stripped me like a tree. They took away my language. This country has a terrible dark history. The blood from those people still runs deep.'

I look at the girl, who is young, maybe 19, to gauge her reaction. But she is strong. Uncle Ivan says he hopes he hasn't upset her by his words. She says she *wants* to know; and that she *wants* to hear from him. And thanks him and goes back to work.

Uncle Ivan turns to me, his eyes pools of mercy and patience. 'Jerrinja!' he says suddenly, startling a bird who is hopping too close. 'That's where we'd get yams, pull them out, roots and all. We always knew when they were ripe, we knew when to eat them. Then there were the chokos. Little wild ones. Ooooh, so yeah, we'd put them on the coals and they were such good tucker. And berries, wild berries. We were saltwater and river people so we got pipis and mussels too.'

I am transported to his life of digging and eating fresh food. It sounds good. So, so good. I ask him how he feels about his children and grandchildren not having the same idyllic life and he explains that 'the whites never listened, no one wanted to know and we were told *to be seen and not heard*.' Uncle Ivan is only a few years younger than my mum but no one ripped away her language and her life.

'When they stopped us using the language,' he says, 'we started to forget the words. So the young ones only get what is left over. We had it all, before other people came here. Sometimes people just want to screw up their eyes and not hear these stories, not see this. It's too much for people to cope with. There's anger there. And you'll feel that anger as you meet us and speak to our people about plants.'

I nod. Uncle Ivan is a well-known and respected spiritual and cultural Elder who has deep experience and a wide view of what has happened. He diverts my attention back to the trees beside us.

'For us,' he says, 'it's what those trees gave us. It's what those trees meant to us. Every tree, every leaf, every seed, every season meant something.'

Uncle Ivan works hard to support the Campbelltown community. He served as a mentor in the Department of Juvenile Justice with 20 other Aboriginal people and still works with local kids as a mentor, helping them stay out of trouble. He gives a huge belly laugh, thinking of the kids in his own family and the trouble they've got up to over the years. His face lights up. 'Prudence, *I* can't talk. I got up to my own fair share of trouble as a kid.'

As we leave the café, Uncle Ivan chats to about eight different people on the way out, calling out 'my uncle' to acknowledge the staff at the Arts Centre. Uncle Ivan leaves me with a warm feeling, like lying on a sunny rock after a swim.

About a week after the interview, I realise I hadn't recorded a single word of our meeting on my phone. And I hadn't asked a single question about plants from my list.

Uncle Ivan had a different story to tell.

LIFEBLOOD: AUNTY SUSAN AND NATALIE

While I was at lunch with Uncle Ivan that day, I bumped into an artist who had been commissioned to make an artwork on the concrete flooring just outside the new herbarium at Mount Annan. Natalie Valiente, a Wiradjuri woman, is a local ceramics artist who has made a number of public artworks and teamed up with established artist, Wiradjuri and Yorta Yorta woman Aunty Susan Grant to collaborate on a public artwork entitled *Lifeblood* for the new herbarium building at Mount Annan.

There is an interesting role for art at the herbarium. There is the history of botanical illustrations, like those of Margaret Flockton. But there are also artists who are drawn to the collection. There are several reasons. First, many artists love archives and collections as much as I do. Second, climate change has meant that artists are critical in mediating these political issues and communicating them in palatable ways to audiences. Third, as soon as you start looking at the herbarium archive, it's hard not to start wondering what Aboriginal and Torres Strait Islander people make of the collection and what it means to them.

At the time of our meeting, Aunty Susan and Natalie's artwork for the herbarium at Mount Annan is yet to be made. Their plans show the concept as an image etched into the concrete floor and pillars just outside the herbarium vaults. The design, of which there are many iterations, has been drawn up by Aunty Susan Grant.

She uses both the botanical image of the eucalyptus and a DNA string to celebrate two cultures – Indigenous and non-Indigenous – and also the DNA of the plants in the herbarium. It represents the complex ecosystems of human and plant life and includes a carved herbarium pole with images of roots going up and forming into tree branches reaching up and out to the Sky People or Ancestors.

In this way all life is connected.

As part of their submission for the project, Aunty Susan's son Cody Leed Evans created a virtual animation of the artwork. This video is a lively and creative contribution to the commission and can be seen on the Australian Botanic Garden Mount Annan YouTube channel. Cody built the assets in the video – the music, the images of plants, the building and visitors – to show how the artwork will be experienced on site. It is due for completion in late 2023.

Natalie and Aunty Susan invited me over for morning tea to tell me more about their work as it connected with the herbarium. So I travel out to Greenfield Park, armed with cakes. Aunty Susan has multiple sclerosis and is mostly confined to a wheelchair, but her home is set up to accommodate her needs and her walls are teeming with her paintings. Several of her ceramic coolamons (traditional trays for collecting) are also in evidence.

We settle in with mugs of tea and the women tell me how there are three circles included in their design which represent the Aboriginal peoples – Dharawal, Gundungurra and Dharug – for whom Mount Annan was a meeting place. The branchlike foliage represents the rivers, creeks and paths that take Indigenous people to their Ancestors.

The artists were inspired by a particular tree at Mount Annan that is intertwined with the tree next to it.

'The DNA represents the first Indigenous people's nation, so that's our blood, so it's life blood,' they explain. 'That links our DNA with our culture and with the spiritual use of eucalyptus, and medicine use, and everything else that is traditional.'

Natalie suddenly disappears and Aunty Susan leans towards me, excited. 'This is amazing,' she says.

'What?' I ask, looking around.

'Wait for Natalie,' she instructs.

Natalie strides back with a few eucalyptus leaves and a small contraption like a pencil sharpener. She plonks the leaves down and places the object on top of them.

'Take a look,' she says. 'Squeeze the light on the side.'

I press the object over the leaf and squeeze the light. It works like a miniature magnifying glass and the image is so clear, like a high-tech x-ray.

'Wow!' I exclaim.

Both women erupt in laughter. 'That's what everyone says,' they cry and hold their sides.

'Where did you get this little magnifying glass? It really x-rays the leaf.' And it does – I can see all the tiny veins of the leaf and all its nodes. The patterns look like rivers and meeting places. It is unbelievable how clear it is.

Natalie grins: 'Got it from a kids' shop.'

This was apparently one of the elements, along with the animated video and detailed concept drawings, that convinced the panel of judges. The artists took two sets of magnifying glasses and strong-smelling eucalyptus leaves in so the judges could experience their idea. Revealing the inner workings of the plant meant their design made complete sense.

Natalie, who undertook the research for the artwork, explains, 'We were looking for information on microscopes, on eucalyptus, and then an image under a microscope, much stronger than this one, and we've gone, "It's the rivers and the tracks that might go through [it]. And then all circles are like the meeting places and the camp sites," so it was like …'

'It's all the places and people,' Aunty Susan says. 'Dharug people go up away from the mountains all the way up to here, and out to like Badgerys Creek and that. And then you got the Dharawal people as well as Gundungurra. So, the artwork design connects to the plant life because of the DNA in the actual plants and also to our First Nations peoples. So, it was very spiritual, very connected. We wanted to make sure it still had the scientific side of things, too. I love the imperfections in the gum leaves, and love doing them.'

Pretty soon, our chat takes a different route. Aunty Susan directs me to a photo on the wall behind me. It's an old, faded photo of a huge tree and she seems to have stuck a piece of bark against the tree, collage-style. She says, 'That was my grandfather's tree down in Narrandera. He cut out the bark to make a canoe. He knew how to cut out the bark so that the tree keeps growing and doesn't die. So that was his tree. And that tree still stands in Narrandera, [that's where] he did all his fishing, and apparently the canoe is in the museum in Narrandera still. So that's something to hold onto dearly. So if you go on the internet, and you search the Canoe Tree, Tommy Johnson's Canoe Tree, it'll come up.'

Susan goes on, 'But my grandfather, yeah. He was a Wiradjuri, but they say that he also may have come from down in Darlington Point, down Hillston, around that way. And he had travelled quite a fair bit because he didn't want to get caught. When they had all their children, they would always load them up in the wagon, and take them down to Albury. We've always moved around.'

Aunty Susan and Natalie exchange a look. 'Stolen generation. They used to take the kids away from families. Sometimes, just picked them up off the street without knowing who they were or who their families were.'

Aunty Susan says, 'My grandmother was at the Warangesda Mission at Darlington Point from 1880 to 1924. She ended up being the cook and served in the main house and stuff. But she was from the Stolen Generation.'

These artists have not only responded to the herbarium collection, but also imbued their design with Aboriginal experiences. Part of the beauty of art is its ability to reconcile and to heal old wounds. I could see that the quiet strands of DNA in their artwork would continue to grow and curl, and their work would tighten and lengthen in its resolve. This was an example of drawing on the richness of the plant archive while also evoking Aboriginal knowledges that sit in the past, the present and also imagines a future.

WHITE DEATH

One of the oldest plants traded across the world is *Saccharum officinarum* – sugar cane. It originated in Papua New Guinea and has a brutal history. Since 1000 BCE this plant has been cultivated across Asia, India and the Pacific. If you've ever held a piece of sugar cane, you'll know the rind can be pulled away and the softer inside bits can be chewed or sucked. Sugar cane was once considered a delicacy.

Nowadays, sugar cane is crushed, its juices boiled and concentrated until crystals form. As soon as humans tasted those sweet, sweet white granules of sugar (also known as white death), their desire became insatiable.

I remember being handed a piece of cut sugar cane as a child during a trip to Queensland. I wasn't very impressed because you really had to chew hard at the tough cane and suck really earnestly to extract the sugary goodness. It was much easier when my elderly neighbour would beckon me over to her house and hand me a whole unpeeled orange with a white sugar cube pressed into a hole in the middle of the orange. I could easily squeeze the whole orange and suck out the juice and sugar. Now that was heaven!

The first documented imperial collecting of sugar cane was by Christopher Columbus in 1493 from the Spanish Canary Islands.[18] The French and British plantations in the West Indies, which started up in Barbados in the 1640s, required huge supplies of labour. Slave labour, trafficked from Africa.

Australia's history does not always make us proud: by 1901 there were still 10 000 Pacific Islander people indentured on

Australian plantations. One of the worst aspects of Australia's sugar cane history is that up to a third of these workers were kidnapped or coerced.[19] Their pay was less than a third of that paid to other workers, and sometimes they were not paid at all.

Sugar was different from other harvested crops because not only had the soil to be hoed and seeds sown, fertilised and cared for, but there was the burning-off of the leaves prior to harvesting, the harvesting itself, and then the processing on site to extract the juice, the boiling and crystallising for sugar. The waste was sometimes turned into rum. Pre-technology, these processes were labour-intensive. And highly profitable.

When I look at the archival photographs of indentured labourers in Australian libraries, there is often a group of Pacific Islander men and women looking completely exhausted. The women seem to be dressed in missionary Western-style clothes (at least for the photographs) and their hair cut very short to the scalp. Some photos show the workers bent double as they cut the cane. Often there is a manager in the photographs, usually in a white shirt, belted pants, high boots and a pale straw hat. Their demeanour is relaxed, sometimes they hold an armful of cut cane or have their arms crossed. Unrushed. Unbothered.

There are stories of white plantation owners giving prizes to whichever worker killed the most rats (a major challenge to the sugarcane crops). There aren't many stories of workers escaping but there are stories of deaths from the extreme work and danger, sometimes multiple bodies would be 'heaped up at the end of the sugar cane field' or just placed in 'a big hole ... as a mass grave.'[20]

But, like so many stolen, oppressed and exploited people, the plantation workers were given a 'ticket to heaven' – a Christian God, and the promise of pleasure, not pain, in the afterlife. As the great Desmond Tutu said, 'When the missionaries came to Africa they had the Bible and we had the land. They said "Let us pray." We closed our eyes. When we opened them, we had the Bible and they had the land.' Hoodwinked.

Sugarcane as agriculture, then, can be thought of as the white death because of the many people who were exploited, undervalued, killed or otherwise ruined by being stolen from their own lands, their own people. Some say that vengeance is giving your enemy poison and wondering why you are sick yourself. However, putting aside the dangers of seeking vengeance, I wonder if the sugar cane itself has sought vengeance on behalf of the people who were enslaved to farm it. After all, Western society's addiction to sugar is considered as dangerous as cancer.

The five specimen sheets for sugarcane (*Poacaeae saccharum officinarum*) in the Sydney herbarium are peaceful, as specimens in an archive usually are. There are 1916 and 1918 specimens from the Richmond River, New South Wales. Two are from near Mackay, Queensland, dated 1955 and 1976. Then we have another of these mysterious places, Guam Experimental Station from the Mariana Islands (spelled Marianne Islands on the specimen sheet) near the Philippines.

In a 1994 report, the Guam Agricultural Experiment Station was working on biological control of whitefly, mealy bug, siam weed and mango tip moth.[21] It seems there are similar facilities around the world, working out of sight to thwart biological criminals. There is now a Western Pacific Tropical Research Center, also on Guam, that includes aquaculture.

So the specimen sheet from the original Guam Agricultural Experiment Station doesn't have a date on the database, but on the photo of the actual specimen sheet, there is a Royal Botanic Garden date stamp of 1918. The specimen includes long swords of sugar cane and a mass of feathery sugar seeds. The other Australian specimens look similar in shape and colour (honey-coloured).

The sugarcane specimens look less like plants and more like offcuts from some messy timber joinery. They certainly do not reveal the violence and abuse in the plant's history. Those horrors are secrets kept within the fuzzy seeds of these specimens. None of the data gives away that truth; you really have to hold your courage and take a deep breath, once those stories are revealed.

DENISE AND THE BLACK BEAN

Like all archives, you have to spend time with them before they reveal their secrets. It's almost like you have to get slightly bored for anything exciting to happen. Don't they say that diligence is the mother of all good luck? I suspect anyone who has searched for something in the library knows what that means. Occasionally, you will be searching for one elusive piece of evidence, only to find something far more exciting instead. This is the luck of the draw. The lucky break. It's true that I have been obsessed with good luck ever since my eldest son battled heart issues as a child. I still give my kids good luck charms before they travel, before their exams, to keep near their beds.

Some plants are collected as lucky amulets. Amulets are objects kept as good or bad luck charms, symbols of protection or curses or cures. Bracelets, coins, armbands, tiny sculpted feet or elephant heads: these are all amulets. They are a kind of sympathetic magic, where an object represents a greater power. I have a substantial collection of amulets at my house and keep them in a small wooden cabinet with glass doors. An example of plant amulets are the sea beans from the monkey ladder vine.

Sea beans, found in the wetlands of the Caribbean and Papua New Guinea, are knocked off their two-metre long vines by monkeys, then fall into estuaries or rivers. The seeds bob along the surface of the water and then get washed out to sea. There, they float around for months and months due to their inner cavities that make them buoyant. Hundreds of thousands of them are bobbing out in the sea right now, only to land on very distant beaches. Perfectly intact.

Around ten years ago, I collected about 12 sea beans from various places. I still have two left in my living room cabinet of curiosities. What was initially interesting about these beans was that they were shaped like love hearts and were known to be collected across many cultures after they fell from the vines. It wasn't and still isn't hard to became obsessed with this idea of seeds as amulets.

The ten sea beans that I no longer have were sent in the mail to friends and family as lucky gifts. I attached a note to each parcel, advising the receiver that the bean seed was a love heart and that I was sending it to them as a token of good luck.

Nine of the ten friends and family rang or texted straightaway, expressing their thanks and saying they loved their good luck love charm. Comforting. They were pretty used to this superstitious behaviour and they also instinctively understood my interest in the force of the gift as a kind of contract of good faith.

But one of the ten people didn't reply and when I next saw this friend and asked if she liked her good luck charm, she wouldn't meet my eye, and excused herself quite quickly. I realised that my gift might have upset her and made her uncomfortable. That friend eventually returned the seed one day. She knocked on my front door and held it out, saying it made her nervous to keep it because she didn't believe in superstitions. Which clearly meant she *did*. Otherwise she would have tossed it in the bin, rather than going to the trouble of returning it.

There is a collection of native black bean seeds that offers a story closer to the heart of the herbarium. These black bean seeds in the herbarium have recently drawn contentious attention. The seeds are similar to chestnuts in size and shape and their pods are like tiny canoes you might keep on the windowsill.

In the field, the seeds of the black bean *Castanospermum australe* are very poisonous to livestock and humans unless prepared and cooked properly. The true story of the black bean was promised to me by the director of the Royal Botanic Garden and Domain Trust, and I was looking forward to hearing her story, which I now consider a kind of gift.

Director Denise Ora has a dynamism and hyper-capability about her. I'd met Denise a number of times during 2019. With dark wavy hair and a chocolate laugh, she is someone you want to spend time with. She has the force of someone who knows what the vision is, how to get there and what that will mean. It is her passion to create a new institute of plant science and her dedication to correcting Aboriginal and Torres Strait Islander erasure from botanical history that sets her apart. Denise advocates for a redress of racism and the colonial structures that continue to burden Indigenous peoples. The black bean is one story of how she is doing that.

On the day of our chat Denise strides along the Royal Botanic Garden's corridor and invites me to follow her through the Sydney building. Through the windows are snatches of exquisite views across the garden and even across the harbour. As I stride to keep pace, Denise calls back over her shoulder. 'My son and I love ancient mythology.' This comment is in response to my garbled chatter about loving history and the stories seeping through the walls of this old building.

As we sit at a table in her office, Denise says, 'We learned about witchetty grubs and boomerangs at school and that's it. We need to introduce [First Nations] language back in and acknowledge a culture that gives different learnings and acknowledge they were the first agriculturists.'

She is right. Education during the 1970s and 1980s consisted of schoolchildren being told that Aboriginal peoples were hunter-gatherers who lived in rock shelters and wore animal cloaks for warmth. This completely contradicts the truth about the ceremonial and spiritual meaning of objects such as emu cloaks, not to mention the inaccuracies of everything we were told. We were fed a story of 'Noble Savages', embellished (by some teachers and family members) with racist slurs, whether intentional or said as off-hand remarks.

Denise's potted history of her time at the helm of the gardens is infectiously enthusiastic: 'One day, I woke up and knew I had to set up an Institute of Plant Science! I wondered how I could make a little bit of difference but I also thought about what we are going to be doing for the next 400 to 500 years, whilst also acknowledging the over 60 000 years of First Nations plant knowledge before that, and how we can do something that creates pride in that history.' Denise is talking about the huge new capital works out at Mount Annan, which includes the now completed new herbarium, preservation spaces, vaults, a nursery for propagation and offices.

Denise tells me that 85 per cent of Australia's plant species are not found anywhere else in the world. She continues: 'Indigenous Australians were constructing dwellings and agriculture and fishing but no one in Australia ever learned about that because it was all destroyed. Over time, we can change the stories and be proud of this culture and that will change the nation, if that can happen. There are so many opportunities in plant science – with food security, propagation, protecting species, healthy landscape. Our

Australian Institute of Botanical Science is putting it all together. We have research horticulturists and education and event spaces – we can share stories and knowledge. I can't fix everything but I can do something.'

And then she starts to tell me about the black bean, *Castanospermum australe*. This inspiring story involved a collaboration between plant scientist Maurizio Rosetto at the Royal Botanic Garden, some PhD students and Indigenous Elders. There is a deep problem with this story, but I'll get to that shortly.

Traditionally, the black bean tree's pods release their seeds and although these seeds and leaves are toxic, Aboriginal peoples understood the nutritional value of the seed, and practised a process of cleaning, washing and cooking the seeds in their leaves so that they were no longer toxic. Then the seeds were crushed to make flour for damper. This all predates white colonisation of the colony. As Denise says, 'It's not the prettiest tree but by god it's clever.'

The research team wondered how the black bean trees had spread from the tip of Cape York all the way down to the rainforests of northern New South Wales. The seeds are too heavy for winds to move and too big for animals to disperse. This mystery initiated genetic analysis of the trees along this route that showed their DNA was connected and suggested that seeds were traded, and travelling with and sharing of seeds was undertaken.

Added to this exciting new development, which contradicts much colonial literature that states that Indigenous people didn't trade or undertake complex land management, was the consultation with Aboriginal Elders who knew the story of the black bean tree and its history. There was an Aboriginal advisory group with representatives from the

Bunya Mountains Murri Rangers, the Tropical Indigenous Ethnobotany Centre and the Firesticks Cultural Burning Alliance.

The Elders gathered extra evidence to complement the genetic research on the black bean. What emerged was information about a Songlines story that supported the story that people carried the plant from place to place. The story follows an ancestral spirit who walked from Byron Bay across the range to western New South Wales with a bag of beans. Together the Indigenous and non-Indigenous researchers drew a map of where they thought the track might have been from Byron across Kyogle and westwards. There, they found more black bean trees that still exist today.

I defy anyone who doesn't get goosebumps from this story of collaborative and cross-cultural research. But there is something that niggles me about the tale as I listen to Denise.

She says, 'That black bean tree was used for food and its glossy leaves were part of that process of making food. Indigenous thinking is circular and they don't put humans on a higher level of importance than trees and it all goes back to mother earth. Our Maurizio Rosetto worked on this genetic research with different mobs and now we know that agriculture was part of Indigenous life for thousands and thousands of years and it was also the start of propagation. It's proven. The research finished in 2019.'

Denise explains, 'The problem with Australia's colonisation was that we were late to be colonised and as soon as humans start to grow crops and keep the surplus, that's when things change. Land clearing and an end to nomadic life … that's when things started to change.'

What's the issue with the black bean story? After all, it's a great story of genetic research and the black bean. Isn't this a truly good news story? Yes. It is. It really is. Having access to genetic testing is critical for showing how plants evolve and move and change. This is so important for understanding everything from plant physiology to changes in climate.

But the thing that's not quite right about this story is that it suggests, or cements the idea, that non-Indigenous Australians need Western science to prove Indigenous knowledge is real or true. The Songlines story was always there. So, there is an argument that there is an ongoing colonial legacy that says modern science needs to legitimise Indigenous knowledge.

Between those Indigenous and non-Indigenous black bean researchers there would have been a huge degree of respect and teamwork. Indigenous and non-Indigenous Australian research was being done together, on equal terms. That is the gift of a project that might also become a lucky amulet. And there will be more of them to find on the road ahead.

DIEFFENBACHIA AND THE HIMMLER STORY

Thinking of plants as gifts is reassuring, but perhaps we should all be a little afraid of plants. There is so much activity happening beneath the bark, beneath the soil, that humans still do not understand.

Plants have a reputation for being benign, generous, benevolent. Many people think of plants as morally 'good'. Maybe they are. But, like humans, they are capable of violence too, even cruelty. Plants can be so amenable, but they can also resist. They can protest and refuse. Plants invade, they steal. Plants overtake and attack. They choke and poison and ... digest.

As humans, we wake up and walk through our days with first-person narratives in our minds. Don't we? Mostly, we are the heroes of our own lives. Those hero-stories are endlessly interesting to us – and to others, if the history of literature, film and television is anything to go by. The world has a thirst for stories, and there are particular human stories that intertwine with plants in ways that are complex and have nothing to do with goodness.

Stories of human violence abound – not least the history of colonial violence against First Peoples. In Australia, there is the violence of land clearing and the resultant loss of biodiversity and the destruction of cultural sites. Other kinds of violence.

Should old violence be met with new violence? Should we burn all of Australia's agricultural industries to the ground because they are compromising the health and wellbeing of the land, the rivers and trees? Should we bomb the coal mines and the fracking pipes because of the disastrous effects of poisoned water tables and irreversible damage to bird and animal ecologies? Should activists raid the monoculture plantations and ringbark them all because lack of diversity starts to diminish the sustainability of those areas? Hmmm, tempting, but perhaps we could find a way that is non-violent.

The second question then becomes: if we don't treat violence with new violence, then, what? Defeat? Surrender? Negotiation? Reason?

Perhaps the best way to redress the violence done to First Nations peoples and their lands rests with timing. Not time, but a particular moment in time. *Kairos* refers to a perfect moment to act. A good way to think of *kairos*, an Ancient Greek word that describes a rhetorical skill, is this: when an archer pulls back her arrow against her bow, lining the arrow up at the target of red and white circles, she holds ... holds ... holds ... until just exactly the right moment. The bowstring is taut but not too taut and the arrow is fixed but not too tight. Then she lets the arrow fly towards the target. That moment. *Kairos*. Timing. The target: better global care for plants.

I think that moment is now. I think plants could unite us. I think the target is in sight. It is time to take better care of plants. But first it would be helpful to get to know them. Allow me to introduce a more violent shade of the plant world to you.

There are two dieffenbachia specimens in the herbarium collection. Dieffenbachia is a tropical flowering plant, often with variegated leaves, meaning they have spots or flecks of white or lighter green on their green leaves. Both herbarium specimens were collected in 1970 from New Caledonia. Both had to be treated for fungal damage and both have labels referring to the Herbarium Museum in Paris. The plants look a little water-logged, as though they never dried out properly. They seem to have been acquired into the collection from Paris, rather than being collected directly.

These specimens are a reminder of the movement of specimens between herbarium institutions for knowledge sharing, for security, for research. It is also a reminder of elite organisations and the often quite establishment, even gentrified, staff who work in these archival institutions. This is an issue being addressed at Kew Gardens in London, who have endeavoured to decolonise their organisation, which includes endeavouring to diversify their staff. Decolonising botanical institutions can also extend to inviting First Nations peoples to give expert advice or to changing the information in their systems to ensure Indigenous protocols are followed and that sacred knowledge is not accidentally shared.[22]

There is an uneasy connection between certain plants and Australia's legacy of colonial history. But that's the perverse adventure of opening drawers and unwrapping specimen sheets. There is a kind of adrenaline rush whenever you go hunting through an archive that has something to do with the possibility of discovery.

One of these stories came to me via a circular garden and a yarn. I first met John Waight online, during lockdown, when I was teaching a research paper course for the Masters of Curating and Cultural Leadership at the University of NSW. This is the best of all courses to teach because the student numbers are small, very small. I love teaching this course. The course involves high levels of one-on-one time with each student to help them write their final paper. Usually the Masters students who take the course are really strong and independent thinkers, so the whole experience is rewarding.

John Waight is a descendent of the Mangarayi people whose Country is just outside Katherine in the Northern Territory. He was in my class of 2021 and he told me plant stories I'd never heard before. At the time he was working for the Black Arts Law Centre; he is now Head of First Peoples Programs at the National Art School in Sydney's Darlinghurst. After the first class when I told the group what my research area was, John couldn't believe that there was such a thing as Critical Plant Studies. He exclaimed and looked like someone had just given him a swag of birthday presents.

'Are you telling me,' he said, leaning into the zoom lens, 'that I can write about plants for this course? Plants!'

Each week, we spent about an hour and a half talking about plants and botanical history. He was reading Plato and Aristotle for pleasure. He was obsessed with gardening. He knew the entire global botanical history of tomatoes. And bananas. This was my kind of student! As with all great students, he taught me more than I taught him. One day, we decided to meet in person because Sydney lockdown had just opened up and there was an interesting exhibition at the Powerhouse Museum of Applied Arts and Sciences, *Eucalyptusdom*, on the eucalyptus tree, which I was reviewing for *The Conversation*.

After we'd seen the exhibition and discussed its strengths and flaws, we sat and chatted. We had a research project in mind for his essay that needed fleshing out. But, as became the case with us more generally, we got distracted by a plant story.

The dieffenbachia. John told me all about this plant, and it's not a pretty tale. The dieffenbachia is known as dumb cane and can be bought all over the place, such as your local Bunnings or Mitre 10. Most nurseries carry it. My local Flower Power, for instance, sells *Dieffenbachia tropical tiki*, *Dieffenbachia compacta*, *Dieffenbachia memoria corsi*, *Dieffenbachia camille*, *Dieffenbachia marina* ... to give you an idea of how many varieties are available just down the road.

The dumb cane gets its name because the leaves are toxic and have been used in another country's shameful history as punishment. The toxins from the plant's leaves make the human tongue swell upon eating. It was used by slave owners in the West Indies to silence slaves, hence 'dumb cane'. It also caused muteness and pain and difficulty breathing. Tucana Indians of the Upper Amazon used the stem of the dieffenbachia for their arrow poisons.

This kind of plant weaponisation gets worse. In Jamaica the dieffenbachia was believed to cause temporary sterility in those who chewed the stem or leaves. By the late 1930s, research had developed and a Dr Gerhard Madaus began testing and publishing the effects of the plant on animal fertility, referring to ethnobotanical folk knowledge.

Madaus owned a company that produced and sold natural medicinals so there might have been a conflict of interest and exploitation of Indigenous knowledge but this story is about the plant. Due to a German interest in 'alternative' medicine around 1920s and 1930s, an unfortunate human–plant relationship evolved.

Nazi SS officer Heinrich Himmler heard of the properties of the dieffenbachia and decided that Madaus' work on animal sterilisation could be a good solution for Nazism's racial and other undesirables. Solution: use dieffenbachia for mass sterilisation. However, Himmler was unable to import enough of the dieffenbachia from South America for his purposes and the project stalled.[23]

John Waight had many more stories about the real history of tomatoes, and about what he sees as the future of the world:

alternative Indigenous plant pharmaceuticals. With anxiety and depression on the rise, new forms of medicines need to be found. John sees the world with plant eyes and makes connections and synthesises information in a very branched way. His passion for plants is not just about the present or the future, but strongly enmeshed in the past.

He told me: 'I am a keen gardener and plant nerd. My mother and family taught me gardening and fostered my interest as a child growing up in the Northern Territory. What I realise is that my experiences in gardening are similar to or exactly parallel to Indigenous people in the Caribbean.[24] Our garden in Darwin, indeed our suburb, was a place of Indigenous trees and shrubs which I will loosely categorise as food, medical, useful and spiritual. They included billy goat plumes, cocky apples, wild passionfruit, paperbark trees and beauty leaf trees.'

John's family also grew bananas, papaws, mangoes, Asian greens, other herbs and spices and ornamentals such as frangipanis, palms and what would be considered house plants. All this was supplemented in the dry season with lettuce, silverbeet, carrots and other plants.

John's family grew these plants well before affordable irrigation systems and air conditioners. Plants were positioned to provide shade from heat and protection from cyclonic winds. Outdoor kitchens were areas to kill and prepare chooks, ducks, guinea fowl, freshly shot magpie geese or fresh fish and other bush food.

His garden was fertilised by collecting seaweed or manure from poultry, rabbits, goats and horses. They did mulching and composting and if it couldn't be mulched it was burnt and spread around. Everything had a purpose; in today's terms it could be classed as tropical permaculture.

When I asked John what he thought about colonial collecting and pillaging, he said, 'I find it quite amazing that these themes relating to the botanical world still exist. There has been botanical commodification through hundreds of years of empire building. Yet it is somewhat erased or conveniently overlooked. Is this because humans' emotional attachment to plants blinds us to look at or question a plant's real history? I now feel on some level I have aided and abetted in some kind of criminal activity when I look at my garden.'

He went on. 'Sydney is a colonial construction, so most garden styles are transplanted from Europe and of course inspired by Mr Monty Don [British horticulturist], but things are changing in this regard. Australia's population is diverse, and our confidence grows, broadening our appreciation of other styles and finally our own identity. Building, gardening, like food, represents our society and it's clear us gardeners and city planners want to make our own mark.'

Does this mean I have, along with thousands of other gardeners, been brainwashed until now? Decolonising is about truth-telling, it is about acknowledging things that are uncomfortable. It's also about recognising how all empires have consequences and have an end!

I talked at length to John about the English philosopher Francis Bacon (1561–1626), who wrote about man's need to master nature, and why 400 years later we have not moved on from these ideas. We still follow colonial protocols of taxonomy and nomenclature – conforming to Bacon's ideas of mastery.

Colonisation is not over in Australia. We haven't done the work yet. We still use the Linnaean plant-naming system at the herbarium. Latin names and common names are mentioned on those beautiful dried and pressed plants, mounted on paper, and annotated with data about where the plants were collected and by whom.

There is still not much mention of the Indigenous people who travelled with early collectors, helping them find tens of thousands of Australian plants. No mention of the lives of the plants themselves either. What did the plants have to say about being ripped out of the ground, cut off trees, yanked and dried, glued and kept? Maybe it's time to think about how Indigenous Australians already knew the names of plants tens of thousands of years before Karl Linnaeus was born.

Maybe it's time to imagine that plants behave in ways that can only be comprehended by contemporary humans as mass distributed intelligence because of the way they share resources, communicate by chemical emissions and thrive in communities.

As John Waight says, the elephant in the room is that all the botanical material is part of the Linnaean system. 'The Linnaean system also now translates to me as [white people] don't know our [Indigenous] history, they could not be bothered to understand us, or they choose to ignore our human connections.'

I asked John if he had any suggestions for decolonising our non-Indigenous relations with plants.

'The most important thing about decolonising is understanding where we position ourselves as individuals in the timeline,' he said. 'For me, I see we have two options: we don't change or acknowledge things and we become lunatics, which I understand as doing the same thing over and over expecting a different outcome … or we change. We learn from the past, adapt our behaviours. If we did, we would all be far more enriched and balanced and become solution-focused. The time we live in, to me, is a grey middle place. Australia is caught between nostalgia and the future on multiple levels. I think gardeners and people who love plants … we are all in this grey area and we are trying to come to a place of balance.'

After listening to John, I pulled out the specimens for dieffenbachia one more time. They are easy to grow as indoor plants and outdoor plants. They are resilient (and toxic). I stared at the specimens on the sheets, willing them to tell me their own story. Now that I knew how malevolently they had been used by humans, I searched the water stains on their leaves and their stubby roots that look a bit like sugar cane for different answers.

But those specimens give away nothing. They are just plants pressed on a page. Perhaps they are innocent victims of human instrumentalism. Perhaps they are conscious – on some molecular level – of the destruction they are capable of. They sit in our living rooms and on our balconies. Pets and kids brush past them, unaware of the secret harm they hold.

As I said at the start of this story, we tend to think of plants only in the context of goodness. Perhaps that is one of the many mistakes humans have made in their relationships with nature. Not all humans are good and not all plants are good either.

PART TWO

PSYCHOACTIVE PLANTS AND THEIR KEEPERS

THE CACAO CEREMONY

It's hard to talk about how clever plants are without sounding glib. It's hard to talk about human relationships with plants without sounding deranged. But a few years back, I was given a substantial quantity of cacao by a shaman friend, and the experience sent me on a plant quest that hasn't ended, as all great quests never do.

The quest was germinated on a hot day in the hinterlands behind Byron Bay. As I approached my friend's 'medicine house', a woman I didn't know lunged towards me and waved a smudging stick in front of my face. The smoke didn't feel very cleansing but maybe that was because the poor woman was dripping with perspiration and had a look of overly earnest intent.

While there were shady trees behind the house, large palms and paperbarks, where we stood at the front was heavy with heat. Once ushered inside the ramshackle wooden house, it was cooler. There were 14 people already sitting in a circle. I didn't know the members of the group and we avoided each other's eyes as we waited to start. People were there for different reasons (curiosity, therapy, a mild high) and at the time I had no idea why I was there at all, except that I had been invited.

My friend, who is also my shaman, watched me closely to make sure I drank the entire mixture. She'd noticed I didn't want to drink it all during the first ceremony a year before. Soon enough, we all settled into our sitting positions. With my eyes closed as part of the group meditation, I started to see colourful patterns. I started to imagine the manky earth beneath my feet. I thought of my toes breaking up mycelium and small roots as I wriggled them.

In this cacao state, I bent down and envisaged soil crumbling on my fingertips. I was conscious and present but I was also somewhere else. Like daydreaming. Or like when you fall into a light afternoon snooze, not quite asleep.

Patterns and forms came across my vision with clarity, as though I'd upgraded my television to high definition. My visions, if that's what I can call them, were almost like children's picture books. Exaggerated and delightful … and simple. I watched animals graze on acacia. I saw a dark form slink away from me, moving off between thick hawthorn bushes. I noticed the tough strength of tree boughs and felt my feet sink deeper into the soil, as though my body was being planted into the earth by a greater force. Cacao is mild and harmless, but it is a beautiful guide towards imagination.

A few weeks after taking cacao, I applied for the grant that began this project. My shaman friend believes the cacao shows us how to look at ourselves, gently leading us where we need to go.

So you could say the cacao has led me here, to this project with the herbarium.

*

There is only one cacao specimen in the herbarium collection. It is *Theobroma cacao*, collected in August 1918 in Viti Levu, Fiji, at the Nasinu Experimental Station. It was later identified and recorded on 25 January 1965. The specimen has wide fat leaves, maybe six leaves in total. In a small plastic bag are two tiny cacao seeds. The leaves look like chocolate. They are shiny, even after over a hundred years of being pinned to the paper, and have the rich colour of milky cocoa.

Of course I want to know what happened out at the Nasinu Experimental Station. I can't find much except that in a *Kew Bulletin* from February 1892 there is a reference to Governor Sir John Thurston setting up a botanic station in Suva, Fiji, to grow agave for fibre. Later sisal hemp was grown. In between those two dates, the cacao was collected.[25]

We might have to use our imagination for what kind of 'other' experiments were being undertaken at the station back in 1918 but there is still a research station there now (funded by the Australian Centre for International Agricultural Research). It appears to deal with invasive species like Koster's curse (a fast-growing tropical shrub) and to have built a biocontrol nursery.[26]

Cacao is a plant with an interesting history of spiritual and medicinal use dating back 4000 years in the cultures of the Incas and the Aztecs (the dried beans were even used as currency by the Aztecs). Cacao too had a history that burgeoned in colonial epochs. By the seventeenth century cacao and chocolate were exotic parts of upper-class European culture. In 1665, Brazil moved cacao plants from the Amazon to the region of Bahia for the benefit of the Brazilian governor-general and to sell any surplus. Even small farms in Brazil continued to grow the crop for centuries. Slavery was not abolished in Brazil until 1888 and the cacao industry thrived for a long time with slave labour from Africa and Papua New Guinea.

Cacao was transported by the Dutch to Sri Lanka and the Philippines, from Guatemala to Spain. Even Jesuit priests around south-east America were harvesting the crop for profit. Then in 1687 Sir Hans Sloane arrived in Jamaica to work as a physician for the colony's new English governor. While there, he noticed locals drinking the cacao bean with water, but he found it too bitter and mixed it with milk and sugar. This was the birth of hot chocolate. Sir Sloane brought the first *Theobroma cacao* 'type' to England from Jamaica.[27]

Thus this ancient plant had cultural associations long before it became a mass produced sweet treat. Over the last five to ten years there has been something of a revival of cacao ceremonies, which brings to mind the problems of non-Indigenous appropriation of cultural ceremonies, partly as a response to people searching for answers in their lives, and partly as our aging populations are becoming more interested in alternative medicines and even microdosing as a means of coping with the pains and illnesses associated with old age.

Whatever the reasons may be, there are widespread inquiries into such alternative spiritual or activated plants at the moment, such as magic mushrooms (thanks in part to the amazing US film *Fantastic Fungi*) and plants that give a mild hallucinogenic experience. Cacao is a stimulant rather than a psychoactive plant, but it can have a spiritual effect, if the environment is conducive. Originally its use was associated with particular rituals and ceremonies. The cacao is rich in nutrients and, like coffee, is a stimulant. The nutrients include iron, magnesium and zinc. It is rich in antioxidants and creates a feeling of wellbeing and happiness if eaten raw or drunk as a mixture with water.

I wouldn't give up the heart-opening visions I experienced using cacao, but I do acknowledge that imbibing psychoactive plants, even the gentle cacao, is serious business and is to be conducted carefully.

Getting to know the cacao increased my awareness of the stories of the plants themselves, not just in the bush but the ones that bubble up out of the plant specimen boxes, that leap off the specimen page and even follow you along the corridors of cupboards and outside into the light. Whispering. They bridge science and human experience, but they also confuse those relationships, which is why I'm desperate to find out more, even the dark-hearted side of plants.

I'd noticed that all the herbarium staff were very disinclined to talk about psychoactive plants in the collection, even mild ones like cacao. There are all kinds of legal and ethical reasons for this. The herbarium does not want to be seen as a place where psychoactive drug-taking can be researched. Nor does it want to put its collection at risk, and some knowledge around drug plants carries risks – the herbarium does not want to be seen to be endorsing risky activities. Fair enough.

WHO CAN ACCESS THE PLANTS?

The herbarium plant archives are a rich resource, a place of intense beauty and significant research. But they are also plagued by cultural erasure and contention. Did they think they could just collect pretty plants, without asking permission – why? Did they think they could create colonial names for plants, without caring what their Indigenous names have always been – why?

This book has been a process of meeting plants in the herbarium collection and working out what their relationship is to the people who care for the plants, the people who research them, and the people who respond to them creatively in the face of cultural erasure. I wanted to find out what other people knew about plants … not just botanical information, but cultural stories and experiences. During my research over the last few years, I regularly asked Indigenous colleagues and other experts I met if they could tell me about Australian psychoactive plants within Aboriginal and Torres Strait Island culture. The response was consistently, no. This was due to secret business and protocol in some cases, and a lack of knowledge in others.

However, I met a group of people I didn't expect to meet. They opened up a whole world of mind-expanding information about plants for me. Meeting this group happened as the result of a zoom call in 2021.

This zoom was just an everyday call as part of my larger research project. One of the artists we commissioned to respond to the herbarium collection was Anna Raupach and she needed access to the herbarium's database in order to make a phone app that responded with sounds and images to the GPS location of about 4000 trees around the herbarium at Mount Annan. Together, the artist and I zoomed with the guy who is responsible for the database and access to it. This is what happened ...

*

Joel Cohen is the senior plant mapping and records officer at the Royal Botanic Garden Sydney. I was surprised by the officiousness of the process to allow Anna access to the herbarium database, which made me feel a bit guarded. I didn't want either of us to have information that might later compromise us, but I also wondered if the security was a bit over the top.

Joel seemed a little wary when Anna and I first asked for the dataset to use for her app. Only when Anna explained that she wasn't using the data for profit did Joel share it with her. This was, of course, Joel's job: to be careful and to minimise risks to the safety of the collections. But it was interesting to discover that the herbarium archive had risks to minimise.

Those risks relate to the location details of plants. Some information is kept confidential. Otherwise, an unscrupulous member of the public might try to access the rich resources of the plant collections for commercial gain. For example, in the past, the latitude and longitude of valuable orchids has been noted by people who accessed the database, and then went and poached the plants from those locations, selling them for a motza.

This seems like a complex problem. Why would anyone want to steal plants or access information about plants when they know they could get caught? How much money is worth the risk of getting caught? And, contrarily, is it ethical to block this information from the public only because it risks poaching? Surely not everyone is a criminal mastermind. What is the point of collecting and keeping all the extra data on plants if it has to be kept a secret?

So I asked Joel to reflect on this for me, because there are elements to the digitisation process that I wasn't familiar with. Apparently the photographing of the herbarium's collection has been the largest digital imaging process in the Southern Hemisphere. Photographically recording 1.4 million specimens and their specimen sheet information is no small task. Mapping and keeping records, which is what Joel does, creates extra information and data. And yet not everyone is allowed to see the data, which suggests a newly created mitigation of perceived risk.

Joel started his botanical career doing biodiversity sampling. After 24 different roles within the Royal Botanic Garden, I think we can assume he knows his way around the organisation, including streams of science, conservation, horticulture, work at the herbarium and experience of the intricacies of complex plant information. His best specialty is 'my fieldwork – the process of collecting'.

His role now is mapping and keeping records of all the living collections. As part of that job, he aims to record over 30 000 trees at the Mount Tomah Botanic Garden in the Blue Mountains. This will require going in and individually accessioning them and estimating their age so that arborists can check on them. The work of assets management, another arm of the Royal Botanic Garden, is to keep an eye on tree limbs so they don't drop on people, so that kind of information would be complementary. All part of mapping and managing.

Joel says that the herbarium is the authority on botanical

names. They review and accept names and publish them once there is a collected specimen. That is the journey of a plant to be considered, identified and known as that plant. The living collection is a little different. The first recorded plant in the herbarium – the type – is rare in the living collections of the Royal Botanic Garden. For example, there is an araucaria species (evergreen conifer trees) type in the living collection in the gardens. A cone was collected on one of the botanist's collecting trips and a seed was germinated from its cone outside in the garden. So it's not exactly a conventional type, because the specimen was taken from a living collection. When this happens, it's called 'of type provenance'. An isotype is the type created if the original type can't be found.

Joel tells me there are laws of propagation bound by the *Biodiversity Conservation Act* of 2016. You need permission from a bureaucrat in Parramatta to collect from a protected area. There are lots of permissions to get through for some plants and the permissions relate not only to threatened species but also to the ecological community in which the plant lives, such as the Eastern Suburbs Banksia Scrub.

I understand that the Eastern Suburbs Banksia Scrub needs to be protected because it is critically endangered, but I feel there is more to this story than Joel is telling me. The best way to find out something that's just beyond reach is to keep asking questions until people pass out. I'm only half joking.

Joel explains that the park rangers work to restrict what you can do, such as sending seeds and plants over state lines. There are some cacti you can't sell, such as *Lophophora williamsii* but nurseries still carry them.

Lophophora is a special plant because of its psychoactive properties. So I ask Joel whether these risk mitigation processes are about stopping people from breaking the law, or more about enforcing the *Conservation Act*. Or if this is actually all about the stigma regarding plants with active psychotropic ingredients.

Joel skips the last parts of my question and tells me that the Botanic Garden has plant-sharing agreements regarding data, but it's hard to police. When someone rings up and requests information, it's hard to know who to trust. For example, some people might come to the gardens to look at eucalyptus trees because they want to compile a field guide. They might take high-resolution images of fruits and buds and gumnuts. But those photographs could then be used by other people to inappropriately harvest seeds. Or they could steal the seeds and sell them on eBay!

Joel gives me another example. 'There might be people who collect plant material for research or are investigating resins for pharmacological purposes. This is far more tricky because it involves wounding the tree to get the keno, the resin.' This strikes me as completely commercial and one to say 'no' to.

It also needs to take into account the ICIP (Indigenous Cultural and Intellectual Property) rights around eucalyptus resin. So these researchers need to seek permission from appropriate Indigenous Elders to do this kind of work with resins. The eucalyptus resin chemical is useful pharmacologically and there are many examples where the published research could go beyond academic interest and into commercial applications.

'And then,' says Joel, 'there are the specimens inside the gardens that have information that should not be shared for fear of poaching or harvesting, such as the cacti that grow in the cactus garden, a couple of which contain mescaline, a psychoactive hallucinogen.' He reminds me that peyotes can be owned but they have the same issue, that of having mescaline as an active ingredient.

My eyes widen.

I have a tiny peyote cactus in my own garden. Actually it sits on my kitchen windowsill. Joel laughs and explains that it's fine, so long as I don't dry the peyote, extract the drug, and use it for a psychedelic preparation.

It wasn't until Joel mentioned the peyote mescaline that I started to understand the risks. That's because, as soon as he told me not to make a preparation from my own peyote as that would be against the law, my immediate thought was *Hmmm, I wonder how that preparation is made*. Human nature. Basic curiosity.

Joel starts telling me about the terrible damage done to the *Acacia cortii* (three brothers wattle), which is really high in DMT (dimethyltryptamine). Because of its hallucinogenic properties, its wild habitats have been badly damaged by people raiding the trees. I start to feel guilty that the idea of peyote production even crossed my mind. So much damage, still.

OK, now Joel has mentioned three types of plants that fall into the 'at risk' category – *Lophophora williamsii*, peyote and *Acacia cortii*. The psychedelics.

Joel assures me that's exactly why these herbarium protections are in place. He promises me that the data of those plants (their GPS locations or anything else compromising) is never shared. Likewise, the location of the ancient Wollemi pines will never be shared. The acacia 'location field' in the database is always taken out when the data is shared, because of the psychoactive elements. He also reminds me that the psychoactive plant community is extremely responsible and its members work hard to shield this information too. That community, Joel says, can also be considered part of plant conservation.

I finish my chat with Joel feeling that a window has opened. A breeze has come in and I am at last comprehending the enormousness of some of these botanical rules and procedures. Joel clearly loves the story of data. He loves finding plants, collecting and noting their soil, how much rain they get, other species close by. He loves propagating plants, choosing the right potting mix and understanding seed coats and how some need to be smoked. He loves the history of these practices. Data is a critical resource, constantly used for interesting analysis, such as different flowering times. The collecting licences are important because they bind everyone to the rules.

But after my chat with Joel, I realised I wanted more information. I had to make contact with the psychoactive plant community. So I spent the next month worrying about how I would do that and what it would mean for me ... and our university-supported project.

COLONISED BY THE PLANTS: PSYCHOACTIVE CACTI GARDENS

There has been a lot of talk, maybe too much talk, about a resurgent interest in natural drug experiences. Mind-altering plants are a critically interesting topic and with it comes all kinds of debates that are useful, so long as they are undertaken with respect, with research and with calm care. As Joel Cohen explained, this trend has had an impact on the herbarium and plant security.

But can we talk about psychoactive plants without endorsing unsafe drug use? Can we discuss the bountiful properties of plants, in all their myriad forms, without setting off fearful social or cultural alarms? I need to find out. Perhaps most importantly, I need to listen to people who work closely with these plants and who advocate for safe relations between different medicinal worlds.

Inspired by the illuminating information that Joel shared, I met the entheobotanical, psychoactive plant community. These are people who work alongside the herbarium and have to grapple with these issues around plant properties every day. But there is a sense at the herbarium that these medicinal and recreational plant associations can be discussed, but not endorsed. This makes sense. But who can talk with me candidly?

What I soon discovered is that, more than anything else, there is an overriding attitude of advocacy and conservation towards plants among the alternative plant community. This adds another dimension to the herbarium specimen collections. I now see those psychoactive acacia and fungi specimens differently. That's how knowledge grows.

So, I decided to get out of my own environment. I swallowed my worries and worked out how to get in touch with the psychoactive plant people. Several members of this community refer to themselves as ethnobotanists (people and plants) or entheobotanists (people and psychoactive plants). I'd heard one of these people give a lecture a while back and so I shot off an email, hoping for the best.

Liam Engel, a cacti expert, replied and agreed to meet me in early January 2022 in the living succulent garden at the Domain, which sits on a high and dry position in the Botanic Garden. Few cacti have been dried and pressed on specimen sheets in the herbarium; they are too large and cumbersome. There are a few kept in the spirit collection, however.

Liam agreed to meet with me to talk about cacti and their characteristics and properties. He has spent time in Mexico and South America learning about cactus culture and has a large collection himself, with an even larger propagating garden.

The day we met was a rainy summer day and rather than standing in the rain, we sought shelter on the steps of the herbarium building. Liam had studied for his PhD in communications with supervisor Professor Deborah Lupton. One of his current mentors is Dr Monica Barratt, who is a social scientist at the Drug Policy Modelling Program, part of Australia's National Drug and Alcohol Research Centre at the University of NSW.

Liam first worked with Monica when researching the Bluelight Forum, an online discussion board where people discuss harm reduction in relation to recreational drug use, with topics ranging from responding to overdoses, to techniques for drug extraction. Monica's work investigates how these social media discussions affect users' health and how official policies should change in response.

Liam said Monica has done fantastic drug research that helps people who use drugs and influences policy reform, working from a position of supporting drug users. An important figure in the drug research field trying to make real change, she helps run the Global Drug Survey, which is not just the biggest drug survey, but the biggest survey of any kind in the world.

Liam is a contributor to Entheogenesis Australis (EGA), an educational entheobotanical and psychedelic non-profit. This is the heart of a community where like-minded research-oriented plant people gather and contribute to education about and communication of plant information, including fungi.

The Entheogenesis Australis team are currently working on a book about common Australian psilocybin mushrooms. Liam is part of this work and wants it to be a waterproof pocket-book that you can carry around, to help lay people understand mushrooms, including how to identify *Psilocybe cubensis*, *Psilocybe subaeruginosa*, *Panaleous cyanescens* and *Psilocybe semilanceata* and their potentially deadly lookalikes.

At the moment, Liam particularly wants to find *Pelecyphora aselliformis* seeds. These seeds grow what some people might call a 'false peyote' – a plant that looks similar to and grows in similar habitats to peyote and might be used as a peyote substitute due to its mescaline content. Liam says, '*Pelecyphora aselliformis* was traditionally used as a peyote substitute and had mescaline in it. It's the only traditionally used peyote substitute that has mescaline in it. So that's why I'm excited by it. It's also super rare and I don't know anyone that has it, and naturally that makes me want it more.'

When I ask why he wants to find the rare peyote he says, 'I'm really interested in peyote cause it's a unique example of the current conservation crisis, while at the same time closely linked with Indigenous communities, psychedelics and drug reform.'

I wonder what Liam makes of the idea of harvesting plants that don't belong to you. Liam says that over time, he's become less interested in what he can take from plants and more interested in what he can give to them. But he thinks it's also the way he treads when he goes on a bushwalk: he is now more concerned about the impact of his feet.

'But will that get to the point where I'm like, "I probably shouldn't bushwalk"? At some point, you do have to make a decision based on what you want. I don't know if that makes it right, but at least if we can own it and try to accept criticism, maybe we can make some progress. It feels like there are two schools of thought on conservation. Either we try to maintain what we have, or we give up and we live in the digital space. And navigating a middle ground between those …'

Liam talks about the problems of decolonising plants. This concept of decolonising plants means one thing for Kew Gardens in London – diversity and access – and another for plant theorists – understanding white privilege and seeking Indigenous expertise. For others, decolonising plants means understanding the significance of the cultural use of plants and who rightly gets to hold copyright of that cultural use.

He says that in the US, members of the Native American Church are permitted use peyote, but it is illegal for anyone else. Some Indigenous communities that have been using peyote for many thousands of years can't officially use it. For Liam, growing cacti, researching illicit plant use and contributing to EGA creates a personal identity.

'I hope that we don't need to decolonise the plant world because we have already been colonised by plants.' Ecological decolonisation can't be led by people, he explains, but instead what we need is a way for plants to represent themselves in human politics.

'Are we working for a human system under the illusion that I am working for the plants, or is that system being used by the plants to popularise plants in human culture? We can't say, and we shouldn't speak for the plants, we need to find a way to let the plants speak for themselves. What will they have to say about vegans? We need human carnivorous plants. That's the only way we can ethically resolve this issue.'

Before we part that day, Liam asks if I'd like to visit some important psychoactive gardens in Sydney. You can imagine my response.

The psychoactive gardens visit

Before I met Liam I didn't even know psychoactive gardens existed. Of course I wanted to see one. I was curious how they might relate back to the herbarium and its remit of care, conservation and research. If the database of the herbarium needs to be protected from plant thieves and other untrustworthy individuals, then were these psychoactive garden people untrustworthy too? Who exactly should we be fearful of, in terms of plant safety?

So on a cool rainy day in February 2022, not long after our first meeting, I drove west to the foot of the Blue Mountains to visit Liam. It took longer than I thought. There is something about Emu Plains at Penrith and even coming back into Toongabbie that is more relaxed than the inner city. Maybe it's the bigger expanse of sky or the wider street verges.

Maybe it's the Nepean River that makes Emu Plains special. The earth smells good out here and you get the taste for a more rural life.

Liam's garden at Emu Plains is abundantly full of san pedros, peyotes and false peyotes. It teems with innumerable seed-grown, cloned and grafted plants. The back garden has a pool surrounded by san pedros.

Liam tells me the conditions are perfect for cactus in western Sydney as the temperature often gets up in the high 40s. I love the native *Callistemon brachyandrus* in Liam's front yard because he has trimmed back all the branches and on some he has nailed round wood pieces and placed cactus on these little stands. The result is a cactus candelabra.

I begin to understand that while Liam presents as a laid-back person with street cred, he also has an extremely sharp eye, and a keen intelligence. He is one of those people whose expertise, experience and knowledge creeps up on you.

Liam has committed a lot of time and passion to being a crusader for safe and informed cactus care and consumption. He is also a gardener.

'This is nothing,' Liam says, as I gaze at all his garden beds and propagation trays. 'Wait until you see the psychoactive gardens I'm about to take you to.'

I have to admit I am excited to see the next two gardens, but I know I can't share their locations or the names of the owners.

We drive for about 20 minutes to meet Liam's first friend. Let's call him Graham (not his real name). Graham has a large backyard with a shed and a greenhouse. He has a forest of san pedros, including what he tells me is called a TBM (*Trichocereus bridgesii monstrose*), otherwise called the 'penis plant' or *frauenglück*, meaning 'woman's luck' or 'happy woman' in German. The origin of this clone is unknown but it has spread throughout the world and I am told it is known for being 'good food' and having potent mescaline content.

Mescaline produces altered awareness, a different sense of time passing, and changes to visual experiences. Sometimes perceptual experiences become enhanced, even euphoric. Some people I've spoken to have had bad reactions such as headaches and dizziness.

Today is a meet-the-mescaline-plants day. Clouds start to cover the garden and a few spots of rain fall. I want to photograph all the cacti. I ask Graham why he started his garden. His answer: 'To eat it all.' He first ate a cactus back in 2014. He had a few dud experiences, both brewing and eating it, but learned to choose the right plants and has grown his own ever since. This is an understatement. His garden has hundreds and hundreds of plants. All in neat rows, some raised up in garden beds. Some eight to nine years old. Many in neat pots that have been grafted or cloned.

I can tell Graham doesn't trust me. I don't really blame him. I don't look like part of the trusted psychoactive community because I'm not. I look privileged, middle-aged, white, a woman. So it's not surprising that he is a little wary, but he offers me a wine.

I decline the wine as I have to drive home for my daughter round 6 pm. But I feel really grateful to be in Graham's garden, even if he keeps casting me sidelong glances. On the one hand, it is like every suburban garden in Australia with mown open lawns (in between the cacti beds), a squeaking metal gate and a red-brick house. On the other hand, it also has a subtle energy. Whatever it is, there is an atmosphere of otherworldliness. It's almost as if the culture of another country has been plonked into a suburban Sydney location. An odd schism of sorts.

While Liam and Graham disappear into a shed and speak in hushed tones as they inspect something within, I wander into the greenhouse on the other side of the garden, which is full to the brim with san pedro with peyotes grafted on top. San pedros are large cacti, with thick stems. Peyote are tiny little button cacti that look like pin cushions.

When they come back, I ask Liam and Graham about these double plants. They explain the peyotes are very slow-growing and so being grafted onto cactus makes their growth rate increase. Plus they look very cool. Graham's greenhouse is in excellent order. Everything is neat and tidy, like the lawn and beds outside.

But Graham is a curious individual who says he wants 'to try loads of different cacti' and 'to brew them all up and see what they are all like'. Liam tells me that Graham is 'Well known and respected for being the *terscheckii* connoisseur because only [Graham] and Peruvian Indigenous people can be bothered to eat that one.' *Trichocereus terscheckii* is known to have mescaline – the active hallucinogenic ingredient for psychoactive experience – but is a much bigger and more difficult cactus to eat or brew than san pedro. Graham cuts out the dark layer of green under the skin, avoiding prickles, and makes a cacti soup.

The greenhouse is full of variegated cactus and it is brimming with propagated plants in pots. There are bags of soil and stone and fertiliser and the air is cool and dry. There are plants from habitat (cuttings, not seed) and there is stuff from the Chacun Chacun tribe of Vilcabumba. Vilcabumba is known as the lost city of the Incas in Peru, at the foot of the Andes Mountains.

Even though we are in Sydney and even though Liam and Graham are not Indigenous people, there is still a strong sense, in this garden, of an older culture, an older place. I can't make sense of it. Much of what makes up the garden has been brought from overseas and sent by express post.

'Don't the drug dogs sniff it out at customs?' I ask.

'Border police are looking for drugs, not plants. You order ten and one might get through,' explains Graham. 'But some of these are old and from Bendigo.'

Bendigo! I marvel that Bendigo was a source of mother cacti, purebreeds.

Graham explains, 'The Bendigo garden is heritage now. Yeah, the owner was a cactus gardener, he got too old, he was a cactus import station back in the day, when it was legal. And they made it heritage, so it's heritage now. In the 1930s, they sent a bunch of people down to South America to collect habitat pieces of cactus, but not long after that it became illegal and you couldn't get anything imported into Australia by Australian law.'

Liam explains that his favourite cactus, the san pedro, is considered to be a weed because it grows in great quantities, whereas peyote is more rare and very slow growing.

Graham breeds his plants, too: 'Yeah, they've got stigma, male and female, you get the pollen and put it on the stigma and yeah, that's hybridisation. And you bag the flowers so the other pollen doesn't get into there. Yeah, you get babies in between two plants. But it's not as easy as it sounds. But the grafted plants, they are not so good for consuming.'

Liam and Graham discuss which plants are psycholeptic (having a calming effect) while I busy myself taking photos and absorbing all the different specimens and species, shapes and combinations.

I feel like I need to give the young people space to catch up. But soon enough Liam is bustling both of us out of Graham's backyard and through his side gate back to the cars. 'Quick, we're late to visit the next garden,' he says.

Before we leave, Graham pulls out some succulent cuttings from a pot near the gate and gives them to me. Maybe he is not so wary of me, after all.

The oldest psychoactive garden

Graham and Liam and I drive for another half hour through the suburbs of western Sydney. This time, eastwards.

I suppose it might be time to wonder why I'm doing this. Why am I roaming around the suburbs of Sydney seeking out gardens of psychoactive plants?

My plant project so far has been to respond to the herbarium collection. That involved our team commissioning poets, filmmakers and artists to respond to plant specimens and to test out the strengths and weaknesses of such collecting institutions. We partnered with the herbarium and also with Bundanon, the old homestead of artist Arthur Boyd, south of Sydney. Bundanon has an exciting remit of environmental art and care. My overall research questions, shared with Bundanon, are about why plants are so important, and why colonial knowledge has left out a chunk of First Nations cultures, and why plant people are so interesting.

It is this last point that is driving me right now. Plant people are special. I had mentioned this to the curator down at Bundanon on one of our zoom calls, and she cried, 'Yes of course they are more interesting!' So I am not alone in my thinking. Plant people are different from mainstream people. This may be because some microdose or imbibe plants for an hallucinogenic experience and know things that others may not. Or maybe it's because they spend so much time caring for plants. Either way, this is the position I have put myself in. That's that.

So it's drizzling with rain as we travel to this final garden but the weather is lovely and cool, especially after a few weeks of intense heat and humidity. I wonder what the cacti make of all the recent wet heat. We can refer to the owner of the next garden as James (not his real name) to protect his identity and also his garden, which is hugely valuable in terms of variety, quantity and dollars. I realise how much of a privilege it is to see these amazing gardens and meet these committed individuals.

So we arrive at garden number three. Again, we have turned up at a lovely suburban house. The front gate has been left ajar, for us I guess, and halfway up the driveway an alarm goes off. I notice a sensor to the right and realise this is some serious security. With good reason, I soon find out. I hope there are no guard dogs and fall in behind Liam and Graham, just in case. If a chunk of flesh is going to be bitten, I'd rather it wasn't mine.

But there are no dogs. A tall man wearing a baseball cap ambles towards us. He has a cactus shirt (so does Liam, by the way) and a gentle demeanour. This is James.

First we move into the heart of the large garden, and pause, naturally gazing up towards a towering tree. Well, it's not a tree. It's a vine that has completely engulfed a tree. A tree and a vine as one! It's ayahuasca, a vine that is growing on a large pine. It's enormous, two storeys high, and its healthy leaves are fluttering brightly in the rainy light of the late afternoon. It is beautiful as it rises up behind the house.

This grand ayahuasca vine is probably near-strangling the pine. The four of us stare up at it in silence. I'm amazed at its excellent condition.

James murmurs, 'I secretly brought a piece of the ayahuasca plant back in my suitcase back in 1993, after visiting Peru. I stayed with a shaman. We slept on dirt and there was no power except batteries for a few hours per day, no electricity. But that guy [he gestures to vine] came back with me in my bag. I was young and silly.'

James lifts up the skirt of the vine to show me the tangle of roots beneath. 'Ayahuasca means divine,' he says. His shaman taught him that the best way to prepare ayahuasca was to cut a length of vine that was the same diameter as the recipient's thumb and then same length as their height. Different tribes do it differently, but that's how he was taught. And that vine was mixed with five to ten *Psychotria viridis* leaves, which have the DMT alkaloid and look a little bit like a marijuana plant.

James shows me a few pots of psychotria he has growing at the back of a small greenhouse. The plants are maybe 60 centimetres high. Apparently these are psychotria hybrids designed to cope with Australian conditions. James had brought leaves of these plants back from South America in his toothpaste container.

Liam, Graham and James start talking about the inbreeding and inappropriate naming of varieties of cactus in Australia. They seem particularly dissatisfied with a plant named 'hope'. I start to look at all James' cacti. Huge old blue ones. Most of his collection is seed grown. He tells me that the v-marks on the cactus show their age. One 'v' is one season of growth. Like the rings of a tree trunk. The gardeners start talking about a large cactus nursery called Hamilton's and how they used to have the oldest and best cactus and peyote but someone tipped them off and plants were stolen.

We move to another part of the garden to see the large greenhouses and stop to talk to James' mother. She is sitting in front of a round prickly cactus in a pot. The mound of cactus is three times the size of one I have at home. With gloves on, she is using huge tweezers to pull out weeds. James' mother is 84 years old and has her hair pulled back in a complex bun. She smiles and seems happy to meet her son's friends. I wonder if she knows how immersed her son is in the psychoactive plant world. Does she approve, turn a blind eye, not really care?

This garden is intense and widespread and must be worth an absolute motza. But James starts to tell me a story that is incredibly important for people who use plant-based drugs. A story that really makes you wonder about the human brain and how connected or disconnected or reconnected humans are, or could be, with plants.

We are standing in his greenhouse, which has state of the art exhaust fans and temperature and humidity gauges and dehumidifiers. James explains that about three or four years ago, 'I had an aneurism. One day I was at work and thought "Something is wrong here." And then my gums were so sore, I had tears coming out of my eyes. And everyone is telling me, "Man, you don't look good. Like, something is wrong. You're really white and you've lost a shit ton of weight." Because I used to be 100 kilos. Anyhow, I said, "Yeah, I'm not feeling well. I'll go home." So before I went to go home, I fainted. So I wake up and they said, "Oh yeah man, go home." So I went home. I was on my way home. I didn't feel good. Mind you, before this, I knew something was wrong so I went to tell the doctors. And they gave me an MRI. But they didn't see anything.'

James went to three doctors. One said it was chickenpox. Another said it was measles. Basically he took himself to hospital twice, to no avail, and kept being sent home. Finally he went back to hospital and had a second MRI and at last the doctors could see the aneurisms and operated, leaving him to recover for six months.

What is so interesting about this story is why James didn't die. Few people survive a brain bleed, and James's was six millimetres by nine millimetres in his communication vein and lasted three days. One doctor believes part of the reason is that James is ambidextrous. The second reason is that they discovered what James had been doing for the three days of brain bleeding, which was agonising and caused intense vomiting and sickness.

He had been consuming constant amounts of mushrooms and cactus and cannabis. Nonstop. He tells us that one of his doctors believed this slowed down the brain and probably slowed the bleed and probably delayed death until they worked out what was wrong.

Of course, this makes me wonder if the magic mushroom, cannabis and cactus caused the bleed in the first place. There is a long history of medicine as cure/kill. Too little, and the medicine is not enough to cure. Too much, and the medicine acts as a poison.

Isn't this the narrative that creates such fear? That we, as consumers, want solutions to our ailments but are wary of the side effects? These issues are true for both approved and unregulated medicines: the impact of certain drugs can't be understood until a later stage. Addictive drugs, such as the analgesic Bex, were not understood for years. Bex was a popular drug in the 1950s and 1960s and it wasn't until 1975 that phenacetin was removed from Bex because it was deemed addictive and could cause kidney cancer.[28] Do these stories strike a chord of terror among mums and dads?

THE CACTUS FAIL

The thing about taking psychoactive medicines is that there are all kinds of risks, including the risk of failure. What happens when nothing happens? Is this a reflection of the plant – that it deems the human subject unworthy of the experience they are looking for? Perhaps some people take these substances but it's not meant to be, it's not their time, the plant decides they are not ready. Or – maybe they dodged a bullet.

I had a friend and her husband over for dinner and was telling them about these amazing secret gardens I had visited and the generous people who owned and cared for them. My friend told me her eldest son had tried to eat a cactus once and had become very sick.

I immediately asked if I could talk to him. They agreed but requested that I use a pseudonym for him – so let's call him Joe. I rang Joe the next day and asked him about his experience. He explained that one of his close mates – let's call him Jason – had been on holiday in South America and, in a Peruvian hostel, had taken san pedro cactus. Jason's experience was euphoric and amazing. Jason had eaten a forearm's length of cactus after taking off the skin and eating the green part above the white matter. This all sounded exactly like the process Liam and Graham had explained.

Jason had told Joe that while it was disgusting to eat, after a half hour the experience had kicked in and was completely joyful. So Joe decided to grow some cactus and thought about eating it. He bought one off eBay and grew it for many months. He had bought it as a san pedro and it seemed legitimate.

Eventually there came the day that he wanted to take it. So he de-spined the cactus, cut off a forearm's length and planned to eat it on a weekend when he was not at work. However, on the Thursday night, he decided to eat a handful of it, just to test the waters. He went to bed and on Friday started to suffer agonising cramps. He had to work but was nauseated and cramped and the pain and exhaustion were insufferable.

By Friday night he called his mother for help and it eventually passed, after much vomiting and pain. I asked if he was disappointed.

'Yes, because my friend had such a good experience so it was a bit of a bummer that I had no psychoactive experience.'

I just had one more question for Joe. Why did he want to take cactus in the first place? There are many other substances that are much less hard work. Joe explained that he was attracted to the idea of working straight with nature. He liked the idea of finding a plant and growing it himself, and then sourcing something directly from nature and preparing it himself. He felt an affinity with the idea of the ritual of preparation and cultural history and feeling connected to the thing that provides a different experience – the cactus.

Joe is not alone. There is a large and growing interest in psychedelics and the reasons are a drug high, medicine, ritual, curiosity, therapy and a natural experience. A combination of these reasons for taking psychoactive plants is often at play.

I am grateful to all these people for sharing their experiences with me. There is a lot of stigma attached to these kinds of activities, which seems to do only harm. Like all negative stereotypes, these attitudes do little more than attract shame and then shameful secrecy. These issues are loaded with politics and the ethics of care.

Ultimately, though, they take us back to the herbarium. Is this information about psychoactive plants included in the data? And if not, should it be? In a way, the herbarium dances around the stigma around psychoactive plants for recreational use. Is that wise? The herbarium wants to reduce harm and avoid injury, of course, but is there a risk that more harm is caused by a lack of information? The herbarium also doesn't want to be seen to advocate these elements of plant–human sociality. Nor do I. But the activity is there. It's not entirely helpful to pretend it's not.

FUNGI FEVER

There has been global fervour around magic mushrooms. Films, television series, articles books have been produced on the subject. Journalist, author and presenter Michael Pollan has popularised these discussions through his book *How to Change Your Mind: The new science of psychedelics*.

An American who seems to be able to talk about these issues without attracting vitriol, Pollan would be surprised to learn how different Australian magic mushrooms are. We have many native mushrooms that have not yet been fully recorded in terms of their psychedelic capacities.

Plants have the capacity to change our minds, to alter our consciousness and maybe even help us become better humans. There are groups of people who do pay attention to the powerful ability of plants and fungi to influence humans in complex ways. So, who are the Australian magic mushie folk, the shroomies?

I contacted Caine Barlow, a mycologist whose particular expertise is in psilocybin-containing fungi. Caine also works with Liam Engel at Entheogenesis Australis. Straight off the mark, he warns me that none of us can wild-collect mushrooms that contain psilocybin. You can look at them, walk around them, and even smell them. But as soon as you lift that magic mushroom from the ground, you are breaking the law.

Caine has a kindly and generous demeanour and runs a group called Guerilla Mycology. He gives talks at institutions such as the University of Queensland. Anything to do with mycelium and psilocybin, Caine knows. He is especially interested in the potential of native psychedelic mushrooms for therapeutic use.

Caine reminds me, before we've even started our chat, that under Australian law mushrooms containing psilocybin, which is a Schedule 9 substance, cannot be harvested. Just in case I've only contacted him to find out where I can harvest free drugs.

He tells me that mushrooms are different from the larger narrative of psychoactive plants. Depending on the state, you can harvest a DMT-containing acacia from the bush, or make a cutting of a mescaline-containing cacti, and these activities are not necessarily illegal – you might be using the acacia for floral arrangements, you may put the cactus cutting aside to plant next spring. Keeping in mind what these plants contain, then intent can itself be a crime.

'Mind you,' says Caine, 'the question is whether you get caught with it, and the context. Or if you get caught with the glassware and the wrong books (or browser history)!'

Hang on a sec. Glassware? Glassware is illegal?

'Not so much illegal, [but] the flasks and extraction glassware for psilocybin mushrooms can be problematic without the right paperwork. Again depending on context.'

I've seen TV series about illegal drugs, like *Breaking Bad*. I don't remember the glassware being difficult to get. But apparently the equipment is restricted because you need special glassware for the extraction process.

Caine says, 'Glassware such as separatory funnels, some condensers, and other equipment require an end-user declaration (an EUD) and proof of identity in order to purchase them.'

A separatory funnel is used when you are mixing different liquids to extract a compound. You shake it, let the liquids settle into their own layer, and drain off either the wanted or unwanted layer depending on your needs. Condensers are essentially like stills (which have their own paper trail!) and can be used to extract oils from which compounds can be further extracted.

It's all about intent. If you are extracting herbal oils, Caine reckons you should be OK – but if you are also found in possession of chemistry books that explain how to extract certain compounds or even books such as *PiHKAL* (*Phenethylamines I Have Known And Loved*) or *TiHKAL* (*Tryptamines I Have Known And Loved*), then it might be a different story.

I wonder about the cactus. Did brewing it require special glassware?

'No, the cactus you can pretty much brew up in a pot. Unless you are specifically after the mescaline. But with acacias, you have to learn how to extract the DMT. And this comes back to intent. In both cases, extracting mescaline or DMT is illegal.'

This is what I love about research. When I woke up that day, I had no idea I would learn about the hardware used for extracting chemicals from plants and fungi. 'Tell me more about the mushrooms,' I say.

'OK, so you can't forage the psilocybin-containing ones. You can't grow them at home because it's also illegal to cultivate them – it falls under manufacture (which includes cultivation) because they contain a scheduled substance. But I should qualify, with foraging, it's also illegal (unless you have a collection permit) to forage any mushrooms from public land, Crown land, or national parks without a collection permit. The *EPBC Act* states you can't collect anything from public land unless you are on a collection permit. So someone who was helping with the Fungimap project, they could go on public land to record species and take notes but they couldn't pick anything.'

Fungimap is a conservation and advocacy site and it is used by the general public. It is a citizen science operation that aims not only to protect the biodiversity of fungi but also to share information. They were shortlisted in 2022 for a coveted Eureka Prize by the Australian Department of Industry, Science, Energy and Resources.

Caine says, 'Coming back to psilocybin-containing mushrooms, currently the only Australian who is allowed to collect magic mushrooms is the University of Queensland's Alistair McTaggart. He has permission from the State Health Department. To culture them, though, he needs a Schedule 9 laboratory, which is locked and all material destroyed after analysis. So for the rest of us, even if you have a collector's permit, you can't pick psilocybin-containing mushrooms.'

I start to wonder about the mushrooms in the New South Wales herbarium and even in the Fungarium (a specific collections area for fungi) over in Western Australia. If psilocybin mushrooms are so difficult to collect, how did they get into the collection at all?

The specimens of mushrooms in the herbarium, just like the acacia and cacti, are carefully protected and not all data information is shared with the public, such as locations of psychedelic plants in the 'wild'.

Caine says, 'The specimens that do turn up at the herbarium are just from old collections – so decades old! And I think that happened because of police confiscating the mushrooms from people that they catch being in possession, then having them identified. Or from someone who's collected it and sent it in wondering what it is, and then it's been identified as psilocybe.

'There is a lot of stigma around this genus. People just don't want to research them because they have to jump through administrative hoops to be able to get the permit to be able to do it. If they want to do any ecological studies, to include psilocybe they have to go through the permit process and then have to have those particular cultures or specimens locked away under the right conditions.'

I think about all this and marvel that we have specimens in our herbaria at all. 'So is private land OK for collecting, if public is not?'

'If you have permission from the landholder, you can forage there. And, if you find something interesting and want to submit specimens to a herbarium, you need a letter stating you have permission.'

'Have you done that?' I ask.

'Well ... I have been caught on private land. I was walking up a community access road and saw some field mushrooms by the side of the road. The farmer saw me, got angry, and yelled at me that I was trespassing and to get off his land. Not that I want to encourage trespassing, but it's almost a rite of passage!'

I realise I haven't asked him which mushrooms are psychedelic.

'So there are the introduced species, *Psilocybe cubensis*, *Panaeolus cyanescens*, and *Psilocybe semilanceata*,' Caine says. 'There are a few other active species that are introduced. But then we have *Psilocybe subaeruginosa*, which is endemic to Australia. *Psilocybe subaeruginosa* is a really interesting case though because its distribution is huge across Australia. There really needs to be some research done on this species, including consultation with First Nations communities. A population analysis of *Psilocybe subaeruginosa* is important to see whether it breaks up into different species or just different varieties, because we don't know. And it's a really, really variable species, so there are a lot of questions.'

I ask Caine about my friends who go mushroom picking and seem confident of their identification abilities. He says there is a definite possibility of picking the wrong species and experiencing toxic reactions, and even death. He has experienced identification problems himself while foraging, finding *Psilocybe subaeruginosa* mushrooms right next to galerinas, which are deadly. Galerina species are known to contain amatoxins, so if you eat enough of those, then you can experience serious bodily harm.

'They look similar?' I ask.

'They can look really similar. The specimens I found, before getting closer, looked the same. But as part of the Facebook communities that focus on active mushrooms, we encourage people who have been out collecting to send us photographs of their mushrooms, and we can identify them as best we can. Other than a few forums such as *The Shroomery* there's few other places you can do that. But as Facebook begins to censor communities, or delete them altogether, people are swapping to other social media, or software. It makes it challenging, and we want to be able to keep people safe!'

What is it about mushrooms that interests him so much?

'It's essentially about that spiritual experience that you kind of have when you head out into the forest,' he explains. 'The "ecodelic" experience. You go out into the forest, and you're wandering along, you might have gone out thinking, I'm just going to go and collect some mushrooms, but you end up discovering how lovely the forest is – it's a refreshing, almost kind of psychedelic space in itself. Definitely, I think my research interest is probably the psychoactive species, but

I really love the edible species as well, but I just love being able to go out into the forest, and upon finding a mushroom it's just like, "Oh yeah, look at you, you're amazing!" I suppose there are maybe four categories, because there are fungi in their own right, fungi for food, psychoactive fungi, but then there's also the medicinal fungi that are not psychoactive. My favourite nonactive is the sea anemone fungus *Aseroe rubra*. They are quite adaptive, I've found them in the rainforest, but I've also found them in wet sclerophyll forests as well. They are now found overseas, in the USA, and were the first Australian species to have appeared in Kew Gardens in London.'

And your favourite active mushroom?

'My favourite active would have to be *Psilocybe subaeruginosa*. Connecting with mushrooms is something that we've been doing for millennia. It's actually part of our human culture to chase spiritual states of mind, and that's what these plants and fungi kind of help with. They're a gateway into altered states of consciousness and the experience of the other, I guess. It means finding the God within, the divine within, and so that's kind of what people are looking for.'

And the plants and fungi give humans that?

'The question is how do the states of consciousness, how do the changes in consciousness, vary between the different plants or fungi that you can ingest to bring on these entheogenic states – alterations in mood, perception, cognition and behaviour? And I guess at a certain point, people find something that maybe clicks with them personally. So some people really do relate to mushrooms, it's just like, that works for me every time, that's what really brings me closer to spirit.'

Caine finishes by saying that 'there is something much deeper that a lot of us are all chasing. We are aware of the recreational stuff, many of us have done the recreational stuff ourselves, and there is a little bit of an evolution in that, in that at a certain point you just find either the spirituality inherent in the experience, or a scientific curiosity about the nature of the experience, or both. How best can I express it? I can take one compound, and I can experience various aspects of myself, and I can take another compound, and I can experience a very different set of aspects of myself.'

Yet again, I am touched by Caine's openness. It constantly impresses me how plant people are open and receptive, curious and adaptable. Caine says, 'Yeah. I guess the point I was trying to get to was just that the community of people in Australia who are interested in the plants, and interested in fungi, have been doing it for a long time; it's a really mature and a really well-educated community.'

Is it counter-intuitive to add that plant people seem to have a different order of care? Is it a counter-narrative to reveal that plant people seem to be more spiritually awake? These are the stories that the herbarium has sent me to, as part of my quest. But they are not stories that are held within the herbarium archives. They are obscured. This is done in the name of protection of the collection and responsibility to the public.

However, there are different ways to look at that aesthetic of care.

PSYCHOACTIVE WATTLE

The entheobotanical community is concerned with cultural plant use, the perception of plants and the capacity of some plants to alter mood, perception, cognition and behaviour. It has its own particular culture. This culture is connected to the botanical world and even to several people who work within the institutions of the Botanic Gardens, although they may not publicly admit it.

In fact, in the same way that gardeners recognise each other by the bit of soil under the fingernails that can't be scrubbed out, so too the entheobots know each other by sight. It might be a tilt of the head or a sparkle in the eye, but there is recognition at play. People know their own people.

This group of informed and experienced plant experts could be described as alternative, even marginalised. They are risk-takers and plant conservators at the same time, which makes a potentially volatile mix.

By that, I mean they work on the edges of mainstream plant science, just outside the established institutions of botanical gardens, community gardens or scientific research. There are interesting debates going on within this community around collecting and using native plants from the bush.

There is also an unspoken war. On one side are people who poach within the psychedelic space for personal gain – the plant thieves. Then there are those who are advocates for conservation and wellbeing – the plant keepers.

Today, I am meeting four of the Entheogenesis Australis

(EGA) crew. I'm grateful they have all made time to talk and wonder if there will be tension between their different points of view.

Caine Barlow and Liam Engel are present, whom I had met before. So is Jonathan 'Ronny' Carmichael, co-founder and president of EGA. The fourth person is known as Darklight. EGA began in 2001 as a small entheobotany network and has grown exponentially over the last 20 years. The EGA website says they offer 'opportunities for critical thinking and knowledge sharing'. There are many other people involved in the Entheogenesis Australis network but this group seems to have a peaceable and collaborative dynamic. They are all passionate about education and health around ethnobotanical plants and psychedelic research and culture. They see themselves as very distinct from the drug baron characters in Australia who are harvesting and propagating plants for big profits.

Caine has a strong warning for those interested in collecting mushrooms as a hobby, whether for food or for psychedelic experience. He says, 'I'm just going to make a little point … You can go out, and you can collect an acacia seed, and you can grow the plant, and you're not going to get into trouble. But if you go off and you collect a rare or psychoactive mushroom and you grow the spores and the mycelium, then you're more likely to get yourself in trouble if you get caught with it. And in that sense, there is another challenge, in terms of plant thief–plant keeper issues.'

Caine is not only advocating for safe and responsible use of psychedelic plants, but also explaining that the group are also avid conservators. They understand the difference between people who have spent a lifetime around plants and people who want to meet a plant only to have a drug experience.

I can already see the difference myself. True plant-lovers have a different way of communicating. It may sound crazy, but it's as though they have learned how to behave ... from the plants.

Caine says that if you obtain a plant, invariably by seed, and you start growing them, then you develop a relationship with them, and then you start to appreciate them. 'People think that, oh I've been growing this plant for five years now and maybe I can harvest it, but then it's just like, actually I don't want to. It develops into this other relationship, this, I guess ... This plant keeper. It's just like, I want to see this grow. I want to see it mature and develop. And then, I guess, we collect its seeds and go from there.'

A popular refrain of the group is that plant thieves can become plant keepers. Many in this community began as plant thieves, in search of therapy or curiosity, spiritual or botanical interest. However, they have all seen the error in poaching from the wild, without care, and all would generally shy away from such actions nowadays.

Ronny talks about discouraging other people from stealing from the wild: 'We can't really influence people [plant thieves] other than try to steer them in a direction, because if we are too hard, they'll push us away. We can't call in the law enforcement. So I guess, we try subtle, more educational, ways to do this. But I honestly think most people who work with these plants pick up energy from the plants and they grow in a better direction, and I feel they naturally come around to this themselves.'

Ronny takes a breath and then continues to explain that it may take someone just politely calling thieves out or recommending alternative sustainable plant sources for them. With that in mind, for many of them, it was a journey they all had to go through. But it's an experiment with a cost. They have all had friends go to jail for working with the plants they love, and they have all had friends die from working in and around this community they are actively all part of. It's risky, and the collectors can be at risk for working with them and possessing them.

Contrary to media stereotypes of drug users, the entheogenic crowd who are interested in the mind-altering capacities of plants and their conservation – and the cultural knowledge associated with them (or the alternative therapies community) – are not a bunch of criminals. They are not criminals in even the smallest ways. They have nothing to do with big drug cartels. This community partners with scientists such as Dr Margaret Ross at the University of Melbourne for drug trials. They regularly consult with Indigenous Elders. In fact, as a group, they have the same characteristics as most people who work with plants.

Entheogenesis Australis also has a sister organisation, PRISM – Psychedelic Research In Science and Medicine – which is undertaking a trial of psilocybin efficacy with St Vincent's Hospital Melbourne. PRISM hosts conferences and symposia with key figures in plant knowledge such as the revered Indigenous author Bruce Pascoe. Art, music and wellbeing are intrinsic parts of the non-profit botanical charity.

Ronny has a long wispy beard and kind eyes. He wears his hair tied back and he speaks gently and patiently. He explains that EGA is basically interested in plant sovereignty, which extends to the politics of sharing and accessibility. EGA's position is that people should have access to plants, and that environmental specifications regarding access need to be understood.

For instance, to grow hemp plants in New South Wales, you need a licence, which is about $200 to $300 annually, and you must receive checks from specialist licensing rangers. The production and selling of hemp products is not legal in New South Wales. These are the kinds of access specifications Ronny is talking about.

What about psychoactive plants?

'We have no problem with psychoactive plants such as mushrooms, acacia or cacti being used to benefit people, but we certainly have a problem with it being done via a for-profit model because we really think that if production is going to happen, the job should be going to people who have a connection with the plant already. Instead of criminalising people with prior plant knowledge, they should be encouraging this expertise,' Ronny says.

There are many people in the EGA community who grow their plants from seed or a seedling, who water and care for plants, who understand their favourite spot in the sun, and understand by smell and colour when is the right time to harvest them. Ronny believes that 'If you can build a connection with a plant, then you're in a much better head space to use that plant for research and as medicine. If that can be done, and if you don't need huge amounts of it, if people can grow those plants in their garden, whether it be using it in a Wiccan context, a healing context or a food context, I don't think you should need a licence if it can be done safely.'

One of the best attributes of this community of EGA people is the clear respect for each other and for the plants. The community may at first appear like a secret society that may or may not be working at the edges of existing legislation. Are they conducting their work for the right reasons? What is clear is that they seem to be securing the future of certain psychoactive plants that are endangered and might otherwise be extinct.

This was the greatest revelation for me, understanding that EGA's broad network of plant-lovers care for the health and longevity of plant species in a very similar way to the plant conservation and restoration groups. In this sense, there is little difference between the EGA crowd and the silver-haired retirees who volunteer at the local botanic garden. In addition, plant people should share 'Caring for Country' responsibilities with First Nations peoples.

Some highly skilled members of the EGA network conduct genetic testing on plant material to ensure the safety of psychoactive recreational drug users. In this way, they work in the same way as public labs or state funded botanic gardens labs, but they do this work at their own expense. They are advancing research in an area that is prohibited by Australia's TGA (Therapeutic Goods Administration), although there may be some changes for the therapeutic use of psilocybin in the coming years.

Before long, Ronny starts telling me about a plant close to his heart and his home: the Mount Buffalo wattle, one of the great acacias that grows in Victoria. This plant has had its populations ravaged by fungal infections and bushfire.

I don't mention this to Ronny, but if I'm honest, this acacia looks a bit straggly. It grows in woodlands and heaths among granite rocks and it flowers in spring. It may not be as beautiful as its wattle relatives but it has a secret ingredient – the psychedelic drug dimethyltryptamine (DMT). It has been cultivated in private gardens in other parts of Australia but its natural remnant vegetation is not strong and needs to be conserved.

Ronny hypothesises that if he was to illegally take even a small number of seeds from the Mount Buffalo wattle, raise them and then propagate additional new seeds, then give those second generation seeds away ... at what point is this good or bad?

This question is an urgent one. The Buffalo wattle is at risk. It could be wiped out by over-harvesting, or by the wasp that has more recently invaded most of the remnant Buffalo wattle bush. Many people in the past who have been interested in the Buffalo wattle for its psychedelic qualities have harvested seed very respectfully and worked hard to continue to grow and care for a plant that isn't available in nurseries. Essentially, these people have ensured the survival of the plant if it was to get wiped out in its original location.

There is another side to this argument. Growing plants in gardens or home labs or even across larger operations is not the same as protecting those trees or plants in their original habitats. Although people may be harvesting seeds and growing them at home and improving the numbers of populations, it is better conservation to leave the seeds where they are and let nature run its course.

Yet another view is that those remnant bush areas no longer exist. Soil erosion, infections, deforesting and invasive species have changed those areas of land anyway. Rewilding, then, is not a legitimate activity, because there is no 'wild' to rewild.

Ronny believes that even though nothing is ideal in relation to the long-term damage non-Indigenous humans have done to natural environments, the idea of plant production, of growing plants and sharing them and getting them into other people's gardens, has a much greater benefit for the plants.

'Like I said at the start, there's many people who collected seeds 20 or 30 years ago, when it was definitely not a negative paradigm to do so,' Ronny says. 'The ideas around biopiracy were not common knowledge back then. People simply collected seeds and they'd grow them and share them.'

I think back to what Ronny said earlier about members of the EGA community doing their own DNA testing. I need to know more. He explains that there are those in the Australian science world who want the psychoactive plant data to stay in Australia.

'They want the research to be done by Australians, but to date I believe a lot of this citizen science has been quite challenging, so people have been bagging things up and sending them overseas because they want the results.'

Ronny thinks that area of citizen science is now turning into largescale bio wellbeing projects. Regular Australians now want to go and collect mushrooms out at some bushy location not too far from the main city centres. Indeed I know several suburban mums and dads who love this activity. They are looking for mushrooms to eat and for mushrooms to have a psilocybin experience.

Of course, as Ronny says, if people go mushroom collecting, they don't want to die from poisoning. So they need to understand the mushrooms and be better able to identify them whether they want to grow them, use them as medication, or even sell them.

It's not just food and an ego-spilling high that people want from the humble mushroom, Ronny says. 'It's certainly flipped from a personal drug interest or a citizen science situation to, now, a mass-scale medical wellbeing deployment. Industry is wanting to know if they can use Australian grown, Australian native mushrooms. Essentially when psilocybin is legal for therapeutic application in Australia [as it is in many US states], then people would like to probably grow it from a local mushroom that is Australian and use that as the medication.'

This is the scary thing about harvesting versus poaching. Who gets to collect? Who gets to genetically test? Who gets to manufacture, to license, to patent, to make money? Should psychoactive plants and mushrooms be decriminalised if they are used as therapy?

Ronny says, 'We completely respect and acknowledge that underground therapy has its uses and is very valuable, and aboveground therapy has its uses and is very valuable too, but we are more interested in how to help people on a mass scale. That would mean reducing law restrictions and criminality. We [EGA] are more interested in a larger picture that actually reduces the pressure on people who are searching for ways to get well. We need a way for us to not be seen as criminals when we're just plant-growers. We would like the law to respect and allow access and use of sacred and medicinal plants.'

It is important to remember that all access and all permissions for the use of plants should also include consultation and permission from First Nations peoples.

Darklight and the whole point of the thing

During our group chat, Darklight speaks from her kitchen table in an undisclosed rainforest location. She looks fierce but calm. I realise for the first time how close we are sailing to illegal activity. This community is not rich. They won't be able to pay tens of thousands of dollars for lawyers if something goes wrong.

In the background of our zoom chat, I can see what looks like laboratory equipment stacked on shelves behind her.

Darklight jokes that she has vials for genetic plant testing in her fridge, rather than food. To me, she appears like many intelligent and eccentric artists I have met in my travels: assured, knowledgeable, capable ... and a little wary of the mainstream world. In effect, she is a scientist.

She has been working with tissue culture and genetics since the late 1990s, and has great respect for Torsten Wiedemann from Shaman Australis. Shaman Australis is the longest-established online community site for ethnobotanists, and Torsten Wiedemann is a hemp and medical cannabis consultant. Darklight explains that he has also worked in clonal propagation (genetic copying) and micro propagation (using tissue samples to grow plant matter) of *Acacia phlebophylla* .... the Mount Buffalo tree again.

Darklight says that if someone asked her to briefly summarise a narrative of the psychoactive community group, it would be that they were educated via the Shaman Australis community forums, found a like-minded community in Entheogenesis Australis and pushed research through PRISM, the psychedelic research charity. She says the flower of all those connections bloomed in their current psilocybin therapy trial at Melbourne's St Vincent's Hospital, whose lead investigator is EGA alumnus Dr Margaret Ross.

In terms of the story of *Acacia phlebophylla*, it's a dual narrative encompassing both psychoactive DMT *and* conservation in the face of climate change. The wasps and rot that are affecting the health of these acacia started to happen over 20 years ago. Torsten Wiedemann supported some early research into the micro propagation in living acacias back in the 1990s. Even then, he was making sure there was enough genetic diversity, so that if something happened, like a fire up on the mountain where it grows, or if the plants all got wiped out by the gall wasps, or an infection was walked in on someone's shoes – and that was a real risk in the early days – then they would still survive.

Darklight tells me how Torsten supported this research financially and academically for three or four years. They went at it pretty hardcore, as did a couple of other tissue culture people, but they didn't get it worked out. They got close, however a few fabaceae are just plain recalcitrant, in Darklight's words, and *Acacia phlebophylla* is one of them. Fortunately, other Australian researchers explored a range of conservation tactics, including improving conventional propagation survival rates, and focusing on other acacia species more amenable to cultivation that have a similar alkaloid profile. These have been successful, and show a multidisciplinary strategy is critical for all conservation work.

This is one of the things I appreciate about this group. They accept that failure and equivocal results are valid parts of the scientific journey. Discussing these openly is key to encouraging younger citizen-science researchers to continue their own enquiries.

Darklight explains that pure acquisition was a really common driver for a lot of them initially. They started out young and perhaps a little irresponsible, but as they learned more (academically or otherwise), talking to people who practised hardcore conservation offered them a broader scope of inquiry that is, in its own way, even more compelling. Many of them began with an intensive interest in the pure compounds for recreational or medicinal reasons and progressed through to wanting a longer-term engagement with those species, their wider biological communities and their interactions with human and economic environments over time.

The plant thieves and the secret species

The four members of Entheogenesis are talking among themselves and I can't quite catch what they are saying. Suddenly, they all start to talk at once. They pause and then begin to tell me about a plant they are not prepared to publicly name. Suffice to say this is another plant that is under threat and there is community and social pressure to harvest it.

Darklight and the others explain that if you go to someone's house out in the middle of a forest and they have a table full of material that they are working on and you can see that it's not the best stuff to be harvesting because that plant is at risk or endangered then you have to call them out. But you can't just abuse them because that won't work and it's better to suggest alternatives that aren't threatened species. You also have to be able to justify why you have a table full of plant material yourself.

Even though there are now lots of alternatives that are less environmentally impactful, this secret plant is now under a lot of pressure. They don't want to publicise the plant, even if it might mean raising positive awareness of its plight. Making it known that the plant needs to be protected will alert poachers who don't really care about conservation.

Liam says that they don't know how many people are involved, but people are cutting down whole trees of this species. They only grow in a small area and are under pressure because they contain the DMT psychedelic ingredient – which is silly considering how many alternatives there are. Additionally silly is that whole trees are being cut down, whereas with this variety you can actually just pick up the fallen flowers and leaves from the ground.

'You don't even need to kill the tree, so the whole thing

is weird,' Liam says. 'I've heard rumours of people who think they know who it is. I reckon it's more than one person, perhaps it's like there's one or two main people that have showed someone else where it grows.'

Ronny points out that it's not all bad news. Through the work of two dedicated tree lovers and community members, this special tree's future is looking up. Around 2014 one EGA member called Sambo perfected a rooting technique from cuttings that proved to be repeatable, consistent and very effective. Then around 2017, another member called Communacacian was able to propagate seedlings at a mass scale and offered acacia conservation workshops. These trees have now been widely dispersed around Australia to ethnobotanical collections and beyond. Collectively, the work of the community has gone a long way in preserving this special tree for future generations, and this work very well may not have happened without interest in the tree's possible medical and spiritual potential.

The herbarium acacia

The herbarium has shared the data on all their collection of *Acacia phlebophylla* plant specimens with me. The database information that herbarium director Hannah McPherson sent me included the acacia longitude and latitude but I won't share that information here, now that I better understand the security risks. The database collection dates give me goosebumps. Why? Because I realise that, in addition to some of the Mount Buffalo acacia being collected in the 1950s and 1960s, I see one date '1 Oct 26' and realise that is 1926! Then I see even earlier ones – 'Sep 1900' and '26 Aug 1880' and '26 Feb 1853'. 1853!

This was an exciting time of scientific discovery in Australia and around the world in astronomy, botany, magnetism and evolution. This was ten years before Georg Von Neumeyer and artist Eugene Von Guerard travelled through the bush from Melbourne to Mount Kosciusko to undertake a magnetic survey of the south-east of Australia. They took a wagon and old barometric, magnetic and weather instruments on a difficult journey with little more than salted meat to eat. Rats were in plague proportions across the area. The 1850s and 1860s was a cruel period of invasion and colonisation, adventure and discovery, of Western scientific research in extremely difficult conditions and of critical Indigenous knowledge systems being ignored or undervalued or stolen.

The earliest *Acacia phlebophylla* was collected from Mount Buffalo National Park in Victoria and was noted as having buds, though no date. The specimen sheet shows a plain brown-phyllode specimen. The phyllodes (leaves) sit nice and flat on the white page. There are some seeds on the cutting, and a phyllode and some seeds have been collected in a sealed little plastic bag. This is often done for the specimens that moult or lose a leaf. There are some added pieces of slightly browned paper that note some corrections, hand-written. Ferdinand Mueller (1825–1896) is the botanist attached to this specimen sheet, which probably means it was sent to Sydney from the Melbourne herbarium, where he was director.

One of the subsequent Sydney botanists corrected Ferdinand Mueller's original name of *Acacia phlebophylla* to *Acacia dallachania*, but in 1981 the correction was changed back to *Acacia phlebophylla*. Painfully, agonisingly, there is another hand-written note so say that 'In Melbourne there is a specimen labelled 'Ferd. Mueller 28/2/18 …' But the last half of the date is covered by another piece of stapled paper. Oh the intrigue! When was Ferdinand Mueller's specimen collected?

I suppose it doesn't really matter that Mueller's specimen in Melbourne might have been collected first. Suffice to say, there is no mention of any psychoactive alkaloids in the database entry.

PSYCHOTHERAPY

In addition to the conservation work of the EGA community, I'm also interested in a second strong aspect of their work: psychotherapy.

The Johns Hopkins Hospital in California has been trialling treatments for addiction, depression, anorexia and PTSD with psychedelics. The EGA people think more phase three trials will be completed within the next couple of years. Dr Margaret Ross is the Australian researcher working on the effects of psilocybin on end-of-life palliative patients. This is psychedelic-assisted psychotherapy. Her work is part of an Australian Research Council grant and takes place at St Vincent's hospital in Melbourne.

Most end-of-life patients who suffer depression and anxiety are treated with medicines or with talking therapies. Some people find these anti-depressant or anti-anxiety medicines make their symptoms worse. In a Q&A with *Psychwire*, Margaret Ross explained:

> Prior to the rescheduling of psychedelic compounds, there were a number of studies conducted using LSD to treat death anxiety of cancer patients with quite favourable findings ... Unfortunately, much of that science was buried with the introduction of the *Controlled Substances Act* and rescheduling of psilocybin globally. Studies in the past decade have indicated quite rapid and dramatic reductions in depression and anxiety symptoms of cancer patients ...

> Being a psychedelic compound, it produces many of the effects that classic psychedelics can produce, including heightened/altered sensory experiences of sound, vision, and bodily sensations, a distorted sense of time, increased sense of empathy and connection to others and the natural world, ego dissolution and mystical/spiritual experiences.
>
> It can also evoke intense emotional experiences, a sense of unity and being 'at one with the universe' (oceanic boundlessness), euphoria … but it can also produce disorientation, anxiety and paranoia in some instances. [29]

This therapeutic work that Margaret Ross has undertaken is moving the psychedelic world forwards. In fact, there has been recent news with respect to psychedelic trials. In February 2023, the Australian Therapeutic Goods Administration approved the use of MDMA and psilocybin for patients under care of psychiatrists. This approval was unexpected and will have significant influence on the psychotherapy field. Caine Barlow says, 'There's also therapy happening in places like Jamaica. So people with money are already doing it [illegally]. They're already going to places where it's legal and they're doing it. But fortunately, the focus is purely on *Psilocybe cubensis*, the most common magic mushroom. So it means then there's no interest in, or little interest in, threatened species.'

I ask this Entheogenesis Australis group what they hope for. They reply that it is to have access to these plants, and not to be criminalised for having access to these plants. This doesn't even include using them. They just want to be able to legally grow and carefully share. And that doesn't move beyond the personal relationships with each other and the plants.

This is not a drug thing for them, but a matter of respecting that these plants have a relationship with humankind and many of them, and in fact most of them, are also associated with altered states or ritual use. Yet they are not looking to alter their states beyond the benefits of tending gardens and botanical spaces. They want to make a better garden, and a better environment that they can relax in, and sit in, and share with other people.

'But,' I say, 'you guys are all at risk because of the psychoactive properties of these plants.'

'Yes,' they reply, 'everything about us is at risk.'

This community is critically important to the herbarium. They are the citizen scientists, the grassroots campaigners for conservation, safety and care. The herbarium, on its own, can't do all this enormous and vastly distributed work. We need community groups with good intentions to help. This includes the Entheogenesis network, the community gardens network and all gardeners at local level, even the guerilla gardeners, whose activism often results in new greening of city spaces.

PLANT DRUG LEGISLATION

What part does the law play in these plant issues, especially now that psilocybin has been approved by the Australian Therapeutic Goods Administration (TGA)? I'm not sure how notions of universal values and societal norms affect plant activities. I'm not sure about the ethics in all of this, at all. Has Australia jumped the gun with early psilocybin TGA approval, before later phase trials were completed? There is a sense, among the plant community, that certain people – big pharma for instance – are going to make a lot of money out of this surprise approval.

Should I think about consequentialist ethics, where any decision is dedicated to the best outcome for the most people, no matter how it is achieved? Or should I think of deontological ethics, which is where the 'right thing' must be done no matter what the consequences might be? It brings to mind the famous trolley car dilemma: a runaway trolley car is heading towards six people, but you can pull a lever and change the course of the trolley so that only one person is killed instead of six. Would you pull that lever?

Interestingly, people – such as my students when we discuss these ideas – always want to know how old the six people are and how old the one person is, to inform their decision. Youth, apparently, is highly prized among the young. I'm always surprised by how many students are deontologic and decide not to pull the lever. They don't want to be responsible for killing one person, even if it means not saving six people. I'm pretty confident I'd pull the lever.

The plant world is riddled with exactly these kinds of dilemmas. Should precious seeds be collected from the wild for propagation and research reasons if the site will be compromised and habitat is at risk, even if it means the long-term survival of that seed? Should we still be using a Western naming system – Linnaean – that is heavy with the burden of colonial crimes, even though it links with other naming systems around the world? Should we have gardens that need watering during drought, even though it improves wellbeing and health? Should we eat plants now that we know they emit emergency signals (compounds) when they are cut?

There is a connection between the plant specimens in the herbarium, collected over decades, and the relationship those pressed plants have to their original locations and what happens next, morally and legally. Which led me to develop my chats with Ronny and the gang a little further. There was also someone else I needed to talk to.

Since 2016 Steve Allsop has been a professor working in the National Drug Research Institute at Curtin University, for nearly half that time as director. He understands the murky ethical areas of the plant drug community. When I speak with him, he observes that whenever high-profile film stars or celebrities go online and talk about their experiences, there is an increase in recreational use. Drug tourism is big business. In Peru, people have set up specialist centres for therapeutic plant medication.

'There is interest in the therapeutic benefits of a range of psychotropic substances,' says Steve. 'Some were set up as psychoactive therapy and now people are starting to re-examine these processes.'[30]

Steve explains that brown tea and jungle tobacco have been used for a very long time, but there are obstacles such as the bioavailability of products and also that a single dose may not be absorbed by the body as the user might want. Brown tea was traditionally used as a medicinal and spiritual tea in South America, but Indigenous people had original knowledge about its efficacy and how to control dosage.

'That's the thing about plant-based drugs,' he says. 'There is the problem of dosage. And also there are new uses now. For instance, 20 years ago no one knew about some psychoactive plants such as acacia. In the past, I have avoided being specific about what types of acacia have psychoactive properties because people go out and start chopping trees down and boiling them up.'

This is a frequent dilemma in the realm of psychotropic plants. Their GPS locations are kept secret by the herbarium and both sides of the psychoactive plant debate (pro-psychoactive plants and anti-psychoactive plants). These groups equally protect locations and even names of new plants found to be high in DMT after new DNA sequencing information has been released.

I ask Steve how many people use or drink acacia. He doesn't know exactly because most of the national surveys face the problem that users don't want to risk criminal prosecution by identifying themselves. Illicit drug users, including users of hallucinogenic plants that they cook up themselves, tend to only talk to their friends. Because of the risks of disclosure, it is hard to estimate the extent of drug use. Even cannabis use is hard to measure. He says that Australia has some of the best survey response rates in the world, but still only 50 per cent of those surveyed respond. The surveys have also historically relied on calls to landlines, often ringing at times when respondents will be out, and mobile phone users are underrepresented. Overall, reported hallucinogenic use is 1 to 5 per cent of the population in Australia and that includes mushrooms and LSD. So not many people.

Many surveys don't drill down and estimate what specific substances might be used as hallucinogens. Steve admits they simply have no idea. There are reports of some hallucinogen tourism to South America – there are over 30 centres in Peru that do drug tours. When researchers try to ascertain why people use them, the answer is that some people are curious, some are risk-takers, some are seeking the euphoria of a high. Then there are others who are on a spiritual quest, who are interested in the history and ritual of the plant. There are those who seek a religious ceremony or even mindfulness, or connecting with history. Finally there are people who are undertaking experimental therapy, guided by a clinician or on their own, because they believe it will help with depression or some other mental health condition. While those populations overlap, it's hard to know what the evidence suggests in terms of numbers, but it's not widespread and probably quite small.

Around five years ago, there were stories coming out of Perth about people harvesting acacia and extracting the DMT in home labs. There were reports of 43 labs in 2015, and even reports of suburban mums taking on the role of backyard chemist.[31] As Steve says, it's hard to assess prevalence of use from the number of labs: a single commercial lab might supply many people, while others might just be supplying a small group of friends or close contacts. So a lab might be conceived of as a 'cottage industry' rather than an industrial-level drug cartel.

Acacia growers and producers may be worried about stigma and discrimination in addition to the more obvious legal reasons when it comes to reporting their activities. If acacia helps users as a medicine, they still might not put their hands up about it.[32] Steve believes plant DMT use tends to be sporadic, compared to people who use cigarettes every day or drink five times per week. For most people it's an occasional activity. LSD users, for example, will rarely use more than once or twice a month. People who drink acacia for therapeutic reasons might use small doses and the challenge is getting exactly the right dose.

Where do they get the plants?

Some people are responsible in their collecting. However, there are reports of some areas outside Perth that have been completely razed, with leaves and branches cut, and roots taken. Steve has not been able to verify these reports.

Is there an anecdotal increase in wild tree manufacturing and use?

There is good reason for plant custodians to be worried. Word spreads and people are searching for an experience, whether spiritual, medical or recreational. There is a long history of using one drug to cure another. Heroin was at times a cure for alcohol dependence, then it became its own problem. The sharing of knowledge on the internet may be a game-changer. Now people are able to look up more information about illegal substances and order online without leaving the comfort of their own lounge room. Steve believes this creates a new challenge – that of large numbers of people experimenting with whatever products are to hand, which can be risky.

'We are seeing changes in drug laws around the world,' he says. This is especially so in relation to cannabis. Across North America there are various forms of regulation from complete prohibition to access to prescribed cannabis for medical conditions to more general access for adults. In Australia we see different responses in different states and territories: from recent legislation in the ACT permitting possession of small amounts for personal use to blanket prohibition in others. Where legislation is changed to allow access to cannabis, we also see divergent laws on how it can be supplied – from no clarity to full-scale commercial production, netting large incomes for large companies. In the case of the latter there is concern that their marketing and supply might not comply with the spirit of laws intended to only apply to low-risk use and promotion.

If people are selling substances in any quantity, then they could find themselves in trouble. Laws in the ACT are complicated – the laws around owning small numbers of plants are there to try and stop people ending up with criminal records just for possessing small amounts of cannabis for personal use.

There is some evidence that the use of nitrous oxide has increased, including heavy use resulting in significant harm. Cylinders of nitrous oxide are readily available for legitimate purposes. Some people have discovered the potential for recreational use and have actively promoted their sale on the internet. This creates a challenge that is readily discernible for all drugs. How do we create awareness of risks while avoiding promoting awareness that results in danger?

There have been attempts to get how-to advice prohibited. There are many people in the plant community who will not divulge how-to information in order to protect plant species and from a concern to conduct themselves responsibly.

Snu Voogelbreinder is an independent researcher in the psychedelic plant space. He gave a conference paper at Tyringham Hall in the UK in 2017 on Australian psychoactive acacia.[33] He noted that in the late 1980s and early 1990s there was increased interest in psychoactive experiences and this began the extraction of alkaloids from acacia. This kind of research was considered illicit and it resulted in the illegal stripping of bark for use and for research. *Acacia phlebophylla* suffered from ringbarking, which was frustrating for plant lovers, because the twigs and branches could also be used – the stripping of bark from the trunk and the cutting of roots was not even necessary. Voogelbreinder was clearly frustrated by the lack of awareness and care for the acacia plants, citing that there were alkaloids other than DMT that could be ingested or vaporised. Stripping the acacia was never necessary. But now, the *Acacia phlebophylla* is at risk.

The moral questions around these issues sit under a cloud of 1970s attitudes. As a child in the late seventies, I remember the fear and even paranoia about drug-taking at the time. There was the threat of insanity, stories of people taking drugs at rock concerts and then jumping off buildings. But these stories were myths in the sense that taking LSD at a music festival did not result in high numbers of users developing a mental illness, just the odd one. But there was a wave of anti-recreational drug use at the time.

The fear spread to marijuana when I was in my teens. There were constant warnings that smoking dope would make you depressed and sofa-bound, would lead to more serious drugs like heroin, would ruin your life. And there would always be an example of some boy or girl who had smoked too much and whose life had been adversely affected. With hindsight, those kids were probably self-medicating for some reason.

The question that remains here is not what to do about drug use, but what to do about plants being harvested from the wild in ways that result in habitat loss and plant extinction. Perhaps the utilitarian doctrine of consequentialist morality is the most relevant. Humans need plants. Plants need diversity and healthy habitats. Humans need to care better for plants.

This will result in the greatest amount of happiness and health for the greatest number of people in an equal way.

This means there should be no quandaries, and if the conservation of habitats and plants relies on psychoactive plant experiences being more legally available to recreational users, then the law as it stands must be secondary.

A proposal to amend the federal *Criminal Code Act* in 2011 that referred to prohibiting not just the extraction of DMT, but owning or growing acacia, was not passed because it was deemed impractical to police the growing of wattle trees in a country where they grow everywhere.[34]

So the rights of the wattle seem to be upheld, for now. No matter that the reason is because of the 'impracticality' of prosecuting the illegitimate extraction of DMT. It makes sense that it would be hard to differentiate between those who grow wattle for the pleasure of having it in their garden and those who grow wattle for psychedelic extraction. Perhaps it is an example of a wicked problem – too vast to be able to solve. Which makes me wonder if citizen science could turn into citizen care, where local groups each protect their little patch of wattle. Is that too idealistic? Or is it a plant contract – one human, one plant. For a healthy plant–human future.

BIOSECURITY AND SHELLEY'S BROKEN WRIST

The herbarium collection has vulnerabilities. The risks relate to the potential of the 1.4 million specimens to be used for individual profit. The herbarium has tight security and within the building itself, the archive is protected in the usual way a museum or gallery store would be, with camera surveillance and access restrictions. It's insured, with safety protocols in place.

I found out about some of the specific risk complexities for the plant collection from Shelley James, who was the manager of the Sydney herbarium collection during one of my early visits when I first peeked into the collection cupboards and the endless red boxes.

More recently, the security questions came up again when in 2019 I made a short film about the glorious bounty of the red boxes full of plant specimens. The film is up on the RBG herbarium webpage and features Shelley James herself. Shelley has pale red hair and gold-rimmed glasses and is smart, knowledgeable and full of energy around the protection and care of the collection. She is now at the Western Australian Herbarium in Perth and recently sent me photos of exquisite and never-ending wildflowers from the Perth hinterlands in springtime.

Anyway, back to the risks. Shelley was showing me some examples from the collection. She had a box that was clearly designed for visitors who wanted a quick overview of the archive. In it were some real goodies. A eucalypt, a kangaroo paw, a daisy, a Wollemi pine ... and a wattle. Shelley pulled out other red boxes to show the extent of the collection, the breadth and the depth, and the overwhelming work of keeping moisture and insects at bay, of keeping information up to date, and understanding that it is a living collection. The resources are regularly pulled out, physically and digitally, for scrutiny by researchers all across the world. What struck me from Shelley's introduction to the herbarium was how universal the knowledge seemed to be and how cooperative all the botanic gardens and herbaria are globally.

As we lingered over the 'visitor folder', we paused on the wattle specimen. Shelley told me that Aboriginal Elders sometimes came in to look at the collection, to check on stories and knowledge they held. We flicked through the sheets one more time, and again she paused at the wattle.

'Shame about some people, though,' said Shelley and then looked sheepish, as though she'd spilled the beans.

This – of course! – intrigued me, so I pushed her a little to explain. She said the same thing that the Entheogenesis crowd had said, that there were loads of people who illegally and thoughtlessly harvested from the wild or even tried to steal from botanic gardens and herbaria. They did this to build rare collections to sell, or to propagate plants you can't get from nurseries, or to get/create hallucinogenic plants.

The obvious problem with this is that rare plants and their habitats mostly need to be protected and conserved and even restored – both in their natural habitats and in the archive. There is also a moral obligation among the botanic gardens community to prevent the abuse of drugs for safety reasons, ecological reasons and biosecurity reasons. Shelley said several *Cannabis sativa* specimens had disappeared from the herbarium collection. One minute they were there, the next, gone. This is specimen theft. Theft from within the herbarium. She also reminded me that there is a legal imperative to protect specimens as the herbarium is bound by the *Narcotics Drug Act*.

Shelley James is no stranger to the power of plants. She had an experience with medicinal plants quite a few years ago when she was in the highlands of Papua New Guinea collecting some of the approximately 20 000 species of vascular plants that grow there. This involved the use of a medicinal plant that released active chemicals, in this case an anti-inflammatory.

The plant was a laportea, a stinging nettle. Shelley was travelling through difficult terrain in the highland mountains, which are notoriously dangerous both in terms of the landscape and in terms of the political situation. On the way back from the expedition, Shelley slipped and broke her wrist. A local Indigenous woman with medicinal plant knowledge made a pulse of the laportea leaves and applied them to Shelley's wrist. Other local women cried in sympathy for Shelley's injury. The leaves kept the swelling and pain down until she was able to descend to the lowlands and seek further medical help.

The descent from the mountain was a two-hour walk and there was an additional three-day wait for the next plane.[35] Once the pulse of ground-up leaves was removed, her wrist swelled up immediately. So the plant had kept the swelling down until the bone could be reset.

What was interesting, Shelley explained, was that for months afterwards the skin on her wrist was 'insanely, irresistibly itchy'. She later found out that the laportea has tiny stinging hairs, no doubt as a defence against over-eating insects or animals. This was interesting to me because it is a reminder of the pharmakon – too little of the cure and it won't work, too much and it can poison.

The laportea that soothed Shelley has leaves like a native hibiscus and tiny little inflorescences that have these clusters of miniature prickles. She never did collect a sample of the plant while this was all happening, which is hardly surprising given the amount of pain she must have been in. The Sydney herbarium, however, already have six specimens of this plant that treats swelling and pain so effectively.

Shelley is steeped in herbaria. In addition to her current role at the West Australian herbarium, she is also a member of the Managers of Australasian Herbarium Collections. This is a subcommittee of the Council of Heads of Australasian Herbaria (CHAH). Its members provide advice and recommendations pertaining to the management of preserved botanical collections. They have more than 18 members and adhere to a 2020 Terms of Reference.

This has become extremely topical of late (even contentious) because the Managers of Australasian Herbarium Collections have had meetings about material that might be offensive, sacred or part of Indigenous ecological knowledge.

As a group, they have conferred. While not all are in agreement, there is discussion about minimising offensive and culturally sensitive information until consultation can take place with the communities, temporarily shielding this information from the public. However, it remains an important piece of the provenance of the collections – part of history and of the collections.

This might strike some people as extreme. Shouldn't we all be able to see what is stored in the database? The information about collection places, collecting people, habitats, any cultural knowledge that has been added? Shouldn't we all be able to make our own decisions about what is offensive? However, the material is still there, stored, at the West Australian herbarium. We just can't freely access it.

Shelley explains that until Indigenous people decide what to do with this cultural information, she believes it is inappropriate to make it available. These decisions should be Indigenous-led, but that work is only now gaining momentum and the privacy and respect for Indigenous people will be upheld until that time.

'Language is owned by the language keepers and that's an internationally recognised human right. So I guess I just felt that until the Indigenous groups decide what they wanted do with their own culture, best that we not share information that can be used against them or taken away from them or used in an inappropriate way. It's still there, it's just in a hidden [database] field. Community may decide that knowledge and language should not be shared. So we just decided that we would remove [certain pieces of knowledge and language] for the time being. I tried to rephrase all the "blackboy" references, for instance.'

Here she is talking about grass trees, the xanthorrhoea, which are a key element of the endangered Eastern Suburbs Banksia Scrub that used to stretch north and south of Sydney. I respect Shelley's calm and open attitude.

I decide to ask one of the harder questions: why isn't tri-naming – adding an Indigenous name to the plant classification system in the herbarium – working? Why do the botanic gardens want it to happen and some Indigenous groups want it to happen ... but it's not happening?

Shelley says, 'If this is a widespread [species], did every community use the plant for the same purpose? Does it have the same name across the species range? How many language groups and communities will need to be consulted to come to consensus? How do you resolve all of that? Tri-naming or penta-naming! So, it's more complex than might be first envisioned. And often there isn't a medicinal use or a name at all.

'It's a tricky situation. I've spoken to taxonomists in New Zealand [Aotearoa] who have been very engaged with community and wanted to use a local Māori name for a species or name it after a person that was part of community ... And it has taken them years to get approval for that word as part of their culture to be used in that way. And so it just ends up being complex. I've got to get this species published because its habitat is threatened. And I've got to get it recognised by Western science. So what can I name it? And so time becomes a factor as well.

'So, I don't know if you're aware, but there's a lot of publications recently in the journal *Taxon*, proposals to change the botanical naming code. Every four years the International Code of Nomenclature is revised, and there are several proposals to change the code that take into account Indigenous naming.'

I realise that what Shelley is talking about is not just adding an Indigenous name. This is bigger! This is changing a Western name into an Indigenous name. This is changing a name that has a negative connotation (for example, the name of a slave trader). There are many stories of cities and towns being renamed.[36]

To digress from plants for a moment, there is the story of the Hitler beetle. Apparently the beetle was named after Hitler in 1933 to honour the Führer; it is a strange little blind beetle. However, neo-Nazis have collected so many Hitler beetles (anophthalmus) from the wild, and even stolen from museums, that the humble beetle is not only blind but nearing extinction.

Naming stories are complex and problematic. As Shelley explains, the nineteenth-century botanist George Hibbert made his fortune from slave trading, forcibly taking African people to new colonies against their will. He was a prominent opponent of the abolition of slavery. Despite this unfortunate legacy, the hibbertia species is a large-scale guinea-flower that grows in abundance in Western Australia. Shelley has more than 9000 specimens of hibbertia in her collection at the Western Australian Herbarium.

At the time, George Hibbert's work was acceptable and to redress the negative aspects of his legacy would mean an unbelievable amount of extra work for the herbarium, such as changing names on each specimen sheet. It would also mean amending the digital data (which would be quicker at least) – and re-educating the public regarding this plant group.

Sometimes these slavery-redress procedures, while moral, are not supportable in an under-resourced sector already struggling to get the basic work done in daylight hours. Shelley says, 'There are rules about naming species to maintain scientific stability, and within our collections a name change means reshuffling everything, renaming everything, database entries modified. So, renaming is not a small matter.'

Shelley believes there needs to be some stability in naming and that perhaps the hibbertia name can be an educational tool to explain the history of slavery and violence wrought by George Hibbert rather than making the story disappear, hiding history.

Before she leaves, I tell Shelley about the exquisite psychoactive gardens I visited west of Sydney. She tells me that she is now also curating the fungi at the Western Australian Herbarium and one of her first jobs was to relocate and secure all the psilocybin and highly toxic specimens in the collection. Unlike Sydney, Perth allows more open access to these collections, so they are still available for study but are given a higher level of protection in a locked room, only accessible upon special request.

When she was looking over the fungi collection, Shelley noticed some of the data was 'a bit weird'. So she asked the previous conservators of the fungi what was going on and they said there may have been some experimentation along the way. Hence the 'slightly weird' data entries.

Shelley is now collaborating with chemists and mycologists to assess the toxicity of native mushrooms. Some look exactly like cooking mushrooms. 'I mean amanita mushrooms can kill you if ingested,' she says. 'Gatherers need to be careful. If you can't be sure of identification, don't eat it!'

PART THREE

REWILDING, CONSERVATION AND CREATIVE REVALUING

THE WILD BANKSIA WOMAN AND REWILDING DEBATES

Picture a woman who stands at her living room window, staring out at a banksia tree. She holds a steaming cup of tea and cocks her head, puzzled. Then she puts down the cup, opens her door and heads out to the banksia tree. She inspects it at close quarters.

Her forehead is wrinkled, not just with time, but also with worry. She does this almost every day and her concern incrementally builds. The tree is a *Banksia serrata*, one of the grandest of the banksia trees. Some people become very attached to their pets. Others get a little too attached to plants and trees. This woman is one of the latter.

She watches this banksia tree over a period of a year, noticing its creamy flowers become increasingly dull round the edges. Later she notices its leaves start thinning out. The tips of its branches seem, to her eye, very brittle (well, more brittle than normal). Even the leathery bark of its trunk seems more lacklustre than the other *Banksia serrata* trees further down the hill that soar up and have bunches of wattle birds pecking at their flowers and bouncing on agile branches.

One morning, after almost a year of watching the tree closely and comparing it to its healthier friends, this woman decides to take action. Some accuse her of being impulsive, of becoming overly consumed by an idea, of rushing things at pace. Slapdash. However, she doesn't really care. Because this problem is strangling her and a year of watching is anything but slapdash.

So she grabs her serrated saw from the back shed, kicks off her shoes and starts to climb the tree. This woman looks slightly mad in her shorts and t-shirt and bare feet. She normally wears a hat but forgets, so her hair frizzes out. She feels like Tarzan but she looks more like a regular city wildwoman.

No one is around, but she wouldn't be bothered anyway. She makes her way up the first few boughs, using only one hand as she's holding the saw. Grunting softly, she moves up quickly and scrapes her right hand, then snags her left shin on a jutting branch. Doesn't notice.

Hanging on with one hand, she leans and hacks at the lower branches that are gnarly and dead. They are brittle, so it's easy to saw. She hoists herself higher and finds a position halfway up the tree. There are loads of dead branches at this level but they are larger, more cumbersome and it's difficult to find a good footing. She saws and branches drop to the ground.

Getting ready to move higher, she slips. Her heart races and her fingers tingle with fear. Falling from the tree would be very bad. She slides down the main trunk and gashes her thigh on a jutting broken branch. The cut is deep and long and it hurts, but she manages to stop the fall near the lower branches. Knowing not to inspect the damage, she moves higher again, ignoring her still-racing heartbeat.

Reaching up, she saws one way, then saws the other. It's not possible to reach the very top branches but there is a ring of dead wood on the ground below her. It's all she can do. Climbing back down is different from climbing up. Perhaps it's the blood dripping from her leg and forearm, or the abrasions on her hand, but her legs have started to wobble.

She jumps down to the footpath from a middle branch because it's easier than climbing down via the bottom branches. Her legs are shaking now. She wants to rake up the dead wood that rings the tree like an extreme haircut, but she fears someone will come along and overreact to her injuries. Leaving the cut wood, she goes inside and puts betadine on her cuts. The thigh is actually really bad but not deep enough for stiches.

She returns to her habit of watching the tree through the window every day. It takes three weeks for her own cuts to heal, and she notices that the tree's cuts are healing too. The sap at all the saw points begins to dry. Together, she and the tree recover.

Eight weeks later, her bruises have turned from purple to yellow and back to normal. She has a scar along her thigh but the other abrasions are gone. Her banksia tree has healed too. New shoots are green and luscious, the whole canopy looks healthy and strong. Later in the year, the creamy flowers look super creamy. And the wattle birds come back too.

*

Conservation is at the heart of the herbarium and it is also what drives most of the plant people who feature in this story. The herbarium specimens are kept so that we know which plants exist, what plants used to grow out in the landscape, and where all these plants still do grow. So the *what* and the *where* are strong currents in the herbarium: we know there are 1.4 million specimens and we know what they are and where they were collected. But why?

This is harder to answer because many great plant collections were originally started as curiosities, then as imperial ambitions increased, so did the desire to amass the best natural history collection in the world. However, the specimens also help us understand climate issues, evolution and genetic changes. There are at-risk plants and communities of plants outside the herbarium. The botanical staff spend time researching and documenting out in the field. They also spend time conserving and caring for plant communities when the bushfires come, as they do more frequently.

One of the issues that is regularly raised is rewilding. There are growing numbers of farmers who are doing regeneration work on their properties such as allowing their rivers and creeks to run more naturally by returning trees to river banks, or by building rocky areas along the creeks to slow the water flow. They allow their fallow paddocks to lie untouched for longer and even realign fields so that there is less erosion and run-off during heavy rains.

It's not just farmers doing this work. There is also interest in permaculture, where ecologies are grown for shade, food and medicine as one incorporated plant model. Groups of Indigenous growers are building ways of farming in traditional ways, such as Bunurong and Yuin man Bruce Pascoe's business Black Duck Foods, which is an Indigenous social enterprise that grows native grains and tubers. Or Bush to Bowl in Sydney.

So the question is this: are these approaches a form of rewilding? Are these rewilding programs at the major botanic gardens (returning the land to its remnant state) feasible? Well, there are two ways of looking at it. First, there is the wish for country to be returned to pre-colonial times, which is a virgin-bush mentality. The problem with this notion of returning to Edenic perfection is that Aboriginal and Torres Strait Islander people were always working the land, so it is not correct to think that pre-colonial Australia was 'untouched'.

The second way of looking at this issue is to remember

that so much of the Australian bush has changed it is perhaps unrealistic to return the land to something that no longer exists. Unrealistic, because the climate has changed, the population has changed, and agriculture and extraction industries have changed the land to such an extent that a return to pre-colonial conditions would not be sustainable.

The third way of interrogating this rewilding question is: should we be interfering with the bush at all? Or even be keeping gardens?

It's hard to know how much to interfere with nature. Despite the heated debate within the communities, it seems difficult to work out exactly how much humans should interfere with plant genetics, or with plant cloning, plant conservation and restoration, with rewilding. How much should that banksia woman have hacked at the defiant banksia tree? Maybe we need to stabilise what is in the bush, alongside conservation and regeneration projects, and then assess.

THE MISSING DAISY
AND LOST SPECIES

On this issue of conservation, the herbarium is not just a site of restoration and genetic research. It is also a place of conservation and regeneration and evolutionary stories. What has been lost, what is missing and what is critically endangered? Could our most at-risk plants be right under our noses?

For many humans, the common daisy is one of the first plants they get to know. Daisies are a regular sight in gardens and by roadsides. Their flower is easily identified with its spongey yellow disks in the centre (stamens) and pretty radiating petals. If you think of a child's drawing of a flower, there you have a daisy.

But if you enter *Paenula storyi*, a particular kind of daisy, into your internet browser, you will not be greeted with a patchwork of colourful flowers shimmering across your computer screen, as you might expect. That's because the paenula daisy has gone missing.

These kinds of stories fill me with anxiety. What, I wonder, have we done to this planet? What horrors are ahead for our children and grandchildren? If our daisies have gone missing, what kind of hope could there be? Is the paenula the answer?

There was an ecologist associated with the herbarium, Robert Story, who collected the only known paenula specimen during a routine collecting trip back in 1961. This plant is one of the hidden stories of the herbarium. The daisy was shaped like a paenula, which was a close-fitting cloak worn on long journeys in Ancient Rome. According to the specimen sheet at the National Herbarium of New South Wales, the paenula collection was made by Story on a hill between the towns of Wollar and Rylestone, four hours west of Sydney.

This hill was rich in deposits of *Nepheline syenite* – a white prismatic cluster of crystals. The commercial value of nepheline is as a sealant and adhesive; it is used in paints and plastics. All of which is decidedly less attractive than the splants that grow upon the hill. Robert Story found the daisy, sampled it and brought it back to the herbarium. When he realised it was not what he had thought he'd collected (according to the specimen sheet he had been looking for a different species, probably belonging to the cassinia genus), it languished in the collection boxes for 40 years, unidentified.

The most exciting part of the herbarium collection is not just the wonderful plants themselves, nor their seed-like fruits in little plastic bags stapled at the top of the specimen sheets or the typewritten scientific names and collection information. It's when you come across a handwritten note by one of the collectors that adds context to the story of the plant, its place, its finding and its history. This paenula specimen is one of those. It has a note from Mr Story, explaining how he collected the fragment and how he realised it wasn't a cassinia but what would be named in 2005 as a paenula. He writes:

> You have all the material there is, but don't worry to distribute any – I feel it is much too scrappy for that …
> I doubt if I'll ever go that way again because it's out of the way and at the end of a very rough track, but I won't forget this plant if I do.[37]

I don't know about you, but this makes me yearn to find that out-of-the-way, very rough track to find more paenula. There is something about Mr Story's last line that *he won't forget* the paenula that suggests it deserves to be remembered.

Marco Duretto is manager of plant diversity at the herbarium. He has examined plant specimens from all around Australia and the world – including South Africa, Kew, Leiden and New Caledonia – to research the herbarium's collections. Most importantly, he often looks at type collections, the specific collections plant names are permanently attached to.

The process of addressing threatened plant species depends heavily on the herbarium plant collection. Duretto cares for the current and historical collections and he says, 'It's important that herbaria continuously add to their collections, as they are a physical and preserved representation of what is growing in the wild, and these collections, old and new, are an incredibly important research tool and not just a static collection.'

He goes on, 'The collection is critical for three things: one, they are a permanent record of what was growing in a particular area and the distribution of species; two, the foundation for documenting our biodiversity, including discovering and describing species new to science; three, an incredible resource to study the evolution of our flora.' Marco and his team conduct research on collection and biodiversity using both molecular data and morphological data.

Specific to the paenula, he is keen to organise a series of field trips to search for this plant and hopefully find a living population. If successful, gardens staff will be able to ascertain the relationships of the species and confirm if it is the only representative of its genus, but to do so he needs to find a series of specimens to tell the whole story.

There is 'no such thing as a new species', he says, just things that are new to science. The paenula genus and its only species were not formally, that is scientifically, described until 2005. The process of naming can take a long time as there may not be a specialist working on that group and so a specimen can sit in the herbarium 'unnoticed' or filed under the wrong name or be simply overlooked. First, a plant cannot be discussed scientifically until it has a name, but once it has been named, the name can be used universally. Second, if a species does not have a name, there is a chance it may disappear in the wild and not be noticed. The conservation status and plans for individual species cannot be assessed or completed without a scientific name. The Australian Plant Census, a working group for the major Australian herbaria, agree on scientific names for Australian plants. The old Cartesian adage *I think therefore I am*, becomes *I am named therefore I am*.

You could accuse botanists and ecologists of playing the master role in their relationship with nature because they limit their official plant research to those that have been named. However, this kind of masterful ordering, this classifying, naming and collecting, is at the heart of the herbarium. It is colonial, yes, but it is also human.

There are problems associated with the masterful and colonial dominion (over Australian land, over our plants, over First Nations peoples), but there is also an exquisite allure to the organisation of all things. This is the attraction of the herbarium, its paradox, which is that there is violence behind the stories of collecting, but there is drama and beauty too.

*

I had the missing paenula on my mind one warm March morning when six of my fellow Dirt Witches picked me up at dawn to go see the pink flannel flowers up at Gooches Crater (which we later christened Gooches Cauldron).

The Dirt Witches is a group of six women – artists, a curator, a writer and a landscape designer – who are activists, creatives, climate change protestors and my collaborators.

Excited plant-talk accompanied me on the two-hour drive: there is nothing like a road trip to reveal more about people. But it's the same with everyone in my life; movement helps them tell me things. Personal things. Philosophical things. Botanical things. Or, maybe movement helps me listen more deeply or with greater attention.

We'd been told the pink flannel flowers had not bloomed since the early 1950s and their extreme florescence was a direct result of the bushfires that had raged through the Newnes Plateau area in December 2019 (although I later found out there was a blooming in 2013 after smaller bushfires). Sixty-eight years (with only one short blooming in between) is a long time for these exquisite flowers to remain dormant, stored in the soil along the ridge line.

As the group of us wandered along the bushy track, astonished at how much damage the fires had caused, how devastated some areas were, from soil to burnt trunk tops, I wondered generally how it might feel, as a plant, to not flower. And also, specifically why didn't the pink flannels flower? Was it too much phosphorus or too much nitrogen? Was it a climate change issue or fewer insect pollinators?

The sea of tiny pink flowers that greeted us was swoon-worthy. This particular species sits low to the ground, and made a heady field of pale pink along the crest of the mountain ridge. I was more used to the north coast white flannel flowers, which are much taller and their flowers larger. White flannel flowers can grow as tall as 120 centimetres – they also flower rarely, and metastasised during the summer after the fires. Newnes Plateau has trigger plants and marsh banksias, wattles and pea flowers.

Down by the creek there was a wort plant that was similar to St John's Wort but more succulent, almost mossy. We all clambered down a curving sandstone platform that was like a steep Triassic slippery-dip. I shimmied down on my bum and almost kissed the earth with relief when we landed at a cave entrance below. There were no pink flannels in this lower part of the crater, and I marvelled that they had chosen such a specific site on the ridge after all these years of being dormant.

My thoughts wandered back to the missing paenula. Perhaps that shy daisy was merely hiding somewhere, invisible to the botanist's eye but biding its time until it felt ready to sprout up or flower. To make itself visible to humans, surely, is a risk for the paenula.

After writing about the paenula, and feeling the weight of a lost flower, it was an enormous relief to see the sea of pink flannel flowers. I was overwhelmed with gratitude that the Dirt Witches had taken me up to see them.

To see flowers that had been hiding was the kind of tonic that deep love brings. It started in my legs as I walked along the ridge beside my Dirt Witch friends and slowly spread up my torso, into my scalp (where it tingled) and then travelled back down to my chest where it sat warm and cosy for days, weeks, months afterwards. I know there is a lot to be scared about in terms of extinctions and habitat loss, but it's always good to see what is there, what has survived, what still thrives.

The mountain track where the flannel flowers grew was easy to navigate but after lunch, the Dirt Witches and I followed another track down by the creek that was rough, scratchy and uncomfortable. It was a thrashing-through scrub rather than a walk and after an hour or two we turned back to gaze on the sea of pink one last time before dusk fell.

Walking that creek track helped me understand what the ecologist Robert Story meant in his note in the herbarium specimen sheet in 1961. There, he said he wouldn't be going back to that nepheline hill near Rylstone any time soon because it was out of the way and a very rough track. I get that. But someone will go back. It might be Marco Duretto or someone else and there will come a time when the paenula reveals herself again. I hope.

FAST EVOLUTION

Have you ever noticed how the sound of the surf gets muffled once you walk over the lip of the first beach dune and down into the swale behind the beach? It's uncanny how the roar can become so quickly muted. Sitting in a sand swale behind the beach, it's calming to watch spinifex grass cartwheel down the dunes.

The endlessly spinning spinifex might continue until the world ends. It looks like the Aristophanes myth: the story of how human life started with a creature that was half-man and half-woman and had four arms and four legs and two heads. Sounds uncomfortable, but apparently these creatures were very strong and powerful. They cartwheeled around (the only way they could move) but Zeus was concerned they were becoming too bold and too threatening, so he separated them into two humans: man and woman. Humans have been searching for their other half – their souls – ever since. The myth is the origin story of heteronormative desire and love.

Spinifex are like those strange multi-limbed creatures. They are so light and their grass-spikes catch onto the sand as they tumble along, slowing their pace. They snag on the bitou bush and the prostrate banksia. The spinifex blows in the wind and they cartwheel in a way that is ageless and timeless and free. But there's a different kind of beach plant that has defied the timeless nature of the coastal dunes.

Arctotheca populifolia is a beach daisy native to South Africa that has done something a bit special. Dr Claire Brandenburger is a digitisation officer at the Royal Botanic Garden in Sydney and has helped coordinate the photographic digitisation of the herbarium's 1.4 million specimens. She also wrote her PhD on the beach daisy.

Like many other plants in South Africa, the little beach flower was picked up by travellers en route to Australia from England, and was brought to Australia in the 1930s as a sand dune stabiliser. In harmony with the spinifex and the creeping succulent pig face, which are native to Australia, the little daisy grew and grew, soon spreading across most of the state's beaches. People mistake it for salt bush but its leaves are a smoky green colour, a little like sage. Its flowers have a yellow central disc (stamen) and bright yellow petals.

The curious thing about the South African beach daisy is that it started to change. Significantly. Over the last nearly one hundred years, the daisy has evolved so fast that it is no longer comparable to its parent population. Brandenburger's research focused on how and why the plant was changing so quickly, and what this could mean for the rapid evolution of introduced species.

She used seeds from the parent population in South Africa (located on Arniston Beach in the Eastern Cape) and planted them alongside seeds from four Australian populations in a common-environment experiment. First, she grew these seeds for one year to produce the next generation, and then she used seeds from this glasshouse-grown generation for her testing and analysis. This process is called 'maternal correction' and accounts for variable conditions experienced by the mother plants of the wild-collected seeds. Over a few years in the glasshouse, and testing around 40 different plant traits, Brandenburger found that in less than 100 years the Australian plant has changed its leaves, flowers, physical and chemical defences, photosynthesis and more!

Brandenburger shares this information in a calm and

informative way but I can't quite get my head around it. So now, the plant powers that be – the taxonomists – have to decide whether this sweet little beach daisy is designated a completely new species. This seems like an amazing transformation to me, and not something to be taken lightly. Humans are generally intolerant of change; we don't appreciate it when friends outgrow us or we outgrow them, when children change and separate from their parents, when couples break up. These are uncomfortable topics in human relations. But everything changes, sometimes drastically, sometimes at high speed. Like the beach daisy.

Should the beach daisy – the *Arctotheca populifolia* – change its name now that it has become so different? We don't know what the new beach daisy thinks about it. So it's most likely irrelevant to the plant. But not so irrelevant to the plant-naming fraternity, for whom naming and classification is a serious business. I can't speak for the beach daisy but I suspect it barely notices the human feet that thump across the dunes. It's probably just enjoying the intensely beautiful Australian sun.

The beach daisy is not especially invasive, says Claire, who ponders the concept of introduced species in the first place. What can we consider as natural movers of seeds? If birds and rivers, then why not humans on boats? She tells me that we must accept that we can't turn back the clock, but we must still do whatever we can to stop any future movement of introduced species around the world. As a South African woman herself, she reminds me that many Australian acacias have become invasive in South Africa. It's important to remember that Australia is not just the depository of all the world's invasive plant species. Our plants are also among the diasporic aliens around the globe.

Before we leave Claire Brandenburger and her rapidly evolving daisy, I should mention again that her team, led by Digitisation Manager Andre Badiou, has been pivotal in digitising the National Herbarium of New South Wales. But there are major challenges with digitising collections that we rarely think about. Generally, the idea that a huge collection will be photographed and made available as part of a huge database is good. Which it is.

However, there are issues of accessibility to herbaria around the world – many have paywalls, so unless you are a member of a botanical organisation you have to pay to access them or cannot access them at all. The herbarium's digitised collection, however, will soon be free for public access.

Another issue is the effort and expense involved in deciphering the hundreds of thousands of handwritten herbarium labels and entering the valuable data they contain onto a database, so that they can be associated with the images that have been taken. These data include fields (or database categories) such as species, location, collector, etc. There is a cost for entering data and the cost is determined by the number of fields. Fewer fields, less expense. More fields, more expense. It makes sense to find a balance and capture the most critical information for each record. However, the problem is that some interesting and important data, for example Indigenous information or naming, just goes in the 'Notes' category ... for now. Hopefully a citizen-science project will help to capture all the data in the future.

Currently the herbarium's database holds 22 records for the beach daisy *Arctotheca populifolia*. The dates of collection range from 1937 and specimens seem to have been very regularly collected through each decade since then, the most recent being collected in 2013. And they were taken from many different places, up the central coast and north coast, and down the south coast from Sydney, plus a few from East Gippsland. What I like about these database entries is the descriptions of where the specimens were found: *on sand dunes; in grassland exposed to sea spray; scattered in white sand; in sandy hollows; nestled among sandy rises.* These are the notes from the plant collectors.

There is something about this beach daisy that has turned our botanists into poets.

BIOPROSPECTING AND THE AFRICAN OLIVE TREES

Bioprospecting, *noun*:

Definition: the search for plant and animal species from which medicinal drugs, biochemicals, and other commercially valuable material can be obtained.

Mount Annan is one of the three Royal Botanic Garden's sites. It sits out at Camden, west of Sydney. As you drive westwards from the city, the traffic offers up more flat-bed trucks and rumbling semitrailers. Time starts to untangle and stretch out to the length of a greener horizon. The temperature rises a few degrees.

Inside the gates, what was once grazing land is no longer pasture. The aesthetic is hard to describe. It's not really *untouched* bush because there are hills of grasses without any trees in sight, save a row of pines. Yet there is Cumberland Plain Woodland still intact to the east of the gardens, which is the original habitat – though carefully restored and regenerated. Mount Annan is not manicured like the Sydney Domain site.

Mind you, there are multiple and highly purposeful plantings all across the site. On its website, Mount Annan refers to 'natural areas' and 'gardening areas'. The gardens are diverse. There are beds of native plants, groves of banksia trees. There are paper daisies and prostrate casuarina. There are teenage Wollemi trees and rainforest plants. There are garden beds full of proteas and waratahs.

The most obvious feature of Mount Annan is the sense of expansive space and a general aura of changeability. The scenery is naturalised, rather than natural. There are ponds with ducks but it's nice and rough round the edges. I've walked over some of the western hills and there are burrs and weeds, but not enough to make me too uncomfortable. The whole site is designed, but there are traces of history. There is a banksia garden, a kurrajong arboretum, ironbark woodland, a callitris (cypress) grove and a bird hide. But it still conjures memories of the original scrub.

Mount Annan has a long botanical history. It bears the obvious colonial fractures of over-clearing and over-grazing, of over-claiming and over-designing. Mount Annan, as a botanic garden, is only around 40 years old, so, as when humans hit 40, there is a mixture of regret and excitement. Young enough to see huge opportunities ahead, old enough to know there may have been errors along the road to get there.

Mount Annan is sign-posted as the Australian Botanic Garden and its landscape has stories to tell about Indigenous knowledges, about changes in land use, about a massive invasion of African olive trees that has left a legacy of plant PTSD.

Softly-spoken Peter Cuneo explains some of that botanical damage and stress to the Mount Annan land. Peter is the manager of seedbank and restoration research at Mount Annan and has an amiability that makes you want to sit on a verandah with some ice-cold cordial and watch the cockatoos soar and squawk. He describes the Australian Botanic Garden as a 'diverse mosaic, a living landscape'. Despite his physical ease, he jumps straight in and starts telling me about bioprospecting, a term I understood as the history of pillaging plants from around the world for utility and for national pride. I was less familiar with it in terms of botanic garden care. Peter explains that bioprospecting has immediate and ongoing legal ramifications for Mount Annan's PlantBank and its archives with respect to who owns the plants and who has the right to collect them, not to mention its obvious moral, ethical and racial issues.

I mention to Peter the 2021 *Manifesto for Change* published by the director of science at Kew Gardens, Alexandre Antonelli, which promised to attend to the history of slavery and racism that occurred (and continues to occur) over the course of Kew's collecting life. Peter's eyebrows pop up because, as he says, Kew Gardens has a 'very colonial persona even up to the recent decade ... very much, Kew is colonial'.[38]

Peter acknowledges that it is really good that Kew makes those decolonial observations and actions, because the ICIP (Indigenous Cultural and Intellectual Property) rights of traditional knowledge is an issue. 'A lot of Indigenous people are not keen on divulging traditional knowledge because it can be used for commercial gain. This makes it a tricky policy area. It's difficult, so RBG must build up trust.'

Peter mentions the Nagoya Protocol, an established agreement regarding the collection and ownership of plants, genetic access and the fair and equitable sharing of benefits from that genetic access. Established in 2014, it is an international legal instrument that was created as part of the Convention of Biological Diversity held in Japan and was intended to create legal certainty and transparency, and to support Indigenous rights.

The way this plays out in Australia is less clear. The Royal Botanic Garden holds scientific licences across New South

Wales to collect plants, activity that is supported by its charter. However, as Peter says, 'What if we collect on Country? Elders will say they own that knowledge.' Who owns genetic material? Nagoya refers to genetic material, and the equitable sharing of that knowledge.

This is where it becomes tricky. Although Indigenous Elders may want to protect the genetic access to plants on Country, there still exists Crown ownership. In other words, in New South Wales, Crown land is ripe for the picking whereas Country is not yet afforded independent status for Aboriginal people to collect material. Peter explains that the RBG had to navigate that conundrum back when they sought to export seed material to the Millennium Seed Bank at Kew a few decades ago. While that process of duplicating seeds as a resource for the future safety and protection of plants makes sense, and is legal in acting on behalf of the Crown as government agency, it also ignores Aboriginal ownership and stewardship.

The issue of genetic material or bioprospecting is huge in Australia, Peter says. People are interested in medicinal compounds of plants as part of traditional pharmacology, and Australia has sought-after organisms, things that grow in extreme environments. So bioprospecting refers to people or companies who go out and collect wild plant material, in many cases without approval or licences to collect. They might be after active pharmaceuticals, and so target areas like the rainforest of Queensland that have a huge diversity of species. Even soil fungi have compounds and they are used as blueprints to develop synthetic chemical compounds.

This is about big business and big profits. It's colonialism all over again!

Peter explains that Australia is such a stable land mass, a

huge diversity of species have evolved, resulting in a unique genetic inheritance in the many different compounds present in our plant life. Australia is now known as a prime site for this kind of pharmaceutical interest. At the Australian Botanic Garden, the interest is less on pharmaceuticals and more on the potential for plants to heal the land through ecological restoration.

This as an area Peter and his team have to work at. Plants like native grasses are important for ecological restoration in areas like the Cumberland Woodland. Seed knowledge needs significant work that can merge Aboriginal knowledges with Western scientific knowledge.

'We need to support seed collection, for example in Indigenous-led ecological restoration and licensing,' Peter says. 'And we need to collect seeds and plants sustainably.'

The African olive tree

Peter Cuneo grew up on the Cumberland Plains in a family of gardeners, so you could say plants were in his blood. He was lucky enough, in his own words, to go to university, the only one in his whole family to do so at that time, and studied science and some biology at Macquarie University. After university, he went to work at the Wirrimbirra Sanctuary at Bargo. This was a native plant sanctuary and nursery in the Southern Highlands. There he met botanist Thistle Harris, who wrote the first books on native Australian plants. She was in her twilight years when Peter met her, and a leading figure in the conservation movement.

Thistle encouraged Peter's interest in native plants and became his mentor. Her knowledge of conservation and native plants during the 1950s and 1960s helped him gain skills in propagation, and Peter ran the Wirrimbirra nursery in the early 1980s. When he heard that Mount Annan was building a new native garden in the mid-1980s, he joined it as chief propagator. So he has been part of the garden from the beginning.

Apart from a few small remnants of the Cumberland Woodland, Mount Annan was cleared pastoral land. Staff have been developing and regenerating it ever since. There were only bare paddocks over the hills in 1986–87. Peter started with the Connection Garden, which was monolithic, built with huge concrete walls and was a microcosm of Australia's entire flora! It was a taxonomic concept – a botanist's dream – but a massive horticultural challenge. He did a lot of plant collecting around Sydney and the region.

In the 1990s Peter led the design and collection development at Mount Annan for ten years. Then he headed up the Natural Heritage section in 2000, which was focused on natural vegetation, restoration, the seedbank and the conservation programs. This involved restoring the woodlands and managing the seedbank across horticulture, ecology and science. For Peter, 'Seedbank has always been a consistent focus since the inception of Mount Annan, and the Millennium Seed Bank [Kew] partnership from 2003 took the seed program to the next level.'

But Peter's best story will always be the African olives.

It happened like this.

A clump of African olives had been planted over in nearby historic Camden Park. The Macarthur family, who owned Camden Park, had imported it as a hedging plant.

'There was a great tradition of that family travelling in the 1800s on the London–Sydney ships, coming round the Cape in South Africa and loading up the boats with African plants. There are records of this. The Macarthurs were great horticulturists and worked out that the African olive was a good plant for droughts.'

There was even a nursery at Camden Park in the 1800s. Olive trees were brought out as a root stock – when you graft another olive onto a hardier root stock that is more disease resistant. They grafted a European olive onto the African olive.

By coincidence, Peter has a big garden at his home in Camden that includes an old hedge of African olive.

He explains that the problem with the African olive is that its small black fruit is prime for bird dispersal, but too small for human consumption. It is biologically very different from Mediterranean olive trees.

'There was genetic work conducted with collaborators in France on the genetics of the original olive trees at Camden Park,' says Peter, 'and they appear to be hybrid. But the ones here are genetically close to the ones on the Cape. We were able to track the origin of these Mount Annan olive trees back to the Cape, hence backing up the story of the Macarthurs. However, we never found an original listing in their archival collection of when the olives brought over from Africa … it just said "olive" on the shipment.'

The original African olive trees at Camden Park are huge. In the 1970s they spread over to Mount Annan. Dispersal would have happened via birds and then they naturalised to their new home and grew and grew. Once they had a critical mass, the population exploded in 1970s. The trees were noticed in Razorback, near Camden, and then at Mount Annan once grazing stopped in the 1980s. By 2000 there were 80 acres of them!

By that time, Peter and his team were focusing on the Cumberland Woodland conservation and tried to get the olives out using roundup and bush regeneration volunteers. They kept it out of there, as a team. Meanwhile, 'Rome was burning' on Mount Annan's eastern ridge. There were remnant eucalypts struggling against a dense olive understorey up there, so they had to start radical mechanical clearing and this caused outrage among the bush regeneration people. But it was the only way to deal with such a dense infestation. This technique used machines to pulverise the trees and left their roots in, so there was no soil erosion, then herbicide was targeted onto the stumps, which has been extremely successful. Peter did his PhD on these olives – he needed to understand the enemy.

The fight against these invasive olive trees is not over but it is now underway. Peter's attitude is about ecology. He seeks to control and restore. There is great value in these ecosystems, such as the connection between the remnant eucalypts and native birds, and it is worth understanding how the olive trees have adapted so quickly. Peter and his team are trying to conserve what was originally there and regenerate other areas, such as the woodlands where the Stolen Generations Memorial is built.

The Stolen Generations Memorial was created to acknowledge the Dharawal people of the Mount Annan area. As a site of healing, it is a place to reflect on the history of forcibly removing Aboriginal and Torres Strait Islander children from their families. Artist Uncle Badger Bates sculpted the sandstone memorial in 2007. This section of bush has a particular atmosphere. It is hidden away from the roads and its quiet serves to make visitors more aware of the natural sounds of the Cumberland bush. It is a significant location for pausing to consider the great damage done to First Nations peoples in Australia.

The ecology of plants involves understanding how plants grow, how seeds behave, what pollinators do, when to collect and how to burn cones.

Peter observes, 'There are some people in our field who say we need to go back to pre-settlement times.'

I ask, sceptically, if that is possible. The wild no longer exists, right?

But all Peter says is, 'It's a great goal.'

HARDENBERGIA AND THE WITCHES FOREST

Hardenbergia is one of 50 species in the ecological cluster that comprises the Eastern Suburbs Banksia Scrub (ESBS). I was part of the Dirt Witches art collective that built a forest in Barlow Street in Sydney's CBD in 2021 that included about 30 of the more than 50 plants in the scrub, including the hardenbergia.

Before choosing the Eastern Suburbs Banksia Scrub, we researched what remnant bush would have been there under Barlow Street. A group of phyto-archaeologists have done extensive research in the foundations of old buildings in Sydney to discover, via soil and pollen analysis, what plants once grew there. Because there was a lack of municipal rubbish collection during the early years of colonisation in Sydney, it's possible to find organic matter from old rubbish pits and foundation fossils. In Haymarket, close to where we grew the forest, there were casuarina and eucalyptus trees, saltbush, native grasses and daisy bush. Nearby there was Chinese bush or *Cassinia arcuate* and *Swamp symphionema*.[39]

In the end, however, we decided to grow an Eastern Suburbs Banksia Scrub. The scrub is a contiguous and endangered group of plants that are part of a particular ecology. The ground cover plants include native geranium, which flourished in Barlow Street. The shrubs include leptospermum, correa and prickly moses, which metastasised in our forest. The banksia trees we planted swayed and climbed higher, although one poor tree had to be hacked back and eventually died. The hardenbergia, lomandra and dianella were soon luscious. Arguably the hardenbergia was the hardiest of all the plants we grew.

When the Dirt Witches grew our 2021 banksia forest, it was structured in a frame of old Sydney sandstone and located in the windswept concrete-jungle street in the CBD of Sydney. The banksia forest was created as a way to connect up with a global movement of micro-forests built in urban locations around the world, as a way to revalue plant life that no longer existed in cityscapes, referencing urban gardener Akira Miyawaki.[40]

The Dirt Witches forest was made permanent by Lord Mayor Clover Moore in 2022 and may inspire other people to grow an Eastern Suburbs Banksia Scrub forest too.

The one Eastern Suburbs Banksia Scrub plant in my back courtyard that I've had trouble growing is the hardenbergia. It is supposedly hardy and easy to grow – indeed it grew well in Barlow Street. But … Not so bloody hardy nor easy to grow in my humble experience.

I tried to grow it in my little greenhouse and it died. I tried it in a pot beneath my frangipani and it died. I tried to grow it out the front in full sun and it died. Eventually, I planted some of the troublesome plant in a bigger garden bed alongside other ESBS plants such as native geranium, snake vine, prostrate *Banksia integrifolia*. And it lived. Actually, it thrived. I guess it just needed some friends.

There are 402 specimens of *Hardenbergia violacea* in the Sydney herbarium. Collected from up and down the coast of New South Wales and Victoria, from islands along the coast, from Leichhardt in Sydney, from Queensland and South Australia. Do I find it even more irritating that this plant is so virulent and extensive, in light of my early attempts to grow it?

Yes. But that's the beauty of plants ... we can't really control them at all.

As I pull up images from the herbarium database, I click on some that have flowers, some that note fruits, one that notes 'sterile'. As these images of hardenbergia pop up in my browser and I click across them, I am shocked to notice something. They have all been preserved on the page in a circular shape. It's astonishing. Image after image shows this unruly plant being remembered in-the-round. Some specimens are clumps, some are crown-like (as the tendrils often get entangled). I love this circularity of the hardenbergia. This must be its natural inclination – I'm confident the botanists didn't arrange any specimens in this way. My favourite specimen was collected from Nora Creek in 1929. It is a little bird's nest of a specimen, snugly curled into a woven ball.

Pre-colonisation, 5300 hectares of Eastern Suburbs Banksia Scrub grew north and south of Sydney, but now there are only 120 hectares left. This is a perfect example of why the specimens in the herbarium are important, to see how the plants have changed and how they grew in the past. There are remnant pockets of scrub at Centennial Park, Queens Park, La Perouse and up on the Manly headland. And, of course, our Dirt Witch forest, which thrives in the windswept city street, helped perhaps by the stingless native bees in the hives we pushed into the corners of the forest.

The hardenbergia at the Dirt Witch forest went nuts. It grew prodigiously at exactly the time my own efforts were failing. It overflowed from the plots we had and waved away down the street. It is a ground cover and important to the scrub because, traditionally, the scrub grows on windswept sandy soil and the trees have only shallow roots. So the ground cover is important to keep the earth stable. This stabilising role is often underestimated. Rather than striving up to the sun like the great tea-trees and banksias, the humble ground cover just creeps along the ground, making sure everyone is safe.

ESBS was well understood by Aboriginal people who gauged how to do firestick farming so that only the understorey of plants was burned back and the flames didn't lick up to the canopy. There have been failed backburn efforts in ESBS bush, for instance out at Manly Head in 2020 when the fire got away from the RFS firefighters and burned the whole headland. When I visited Manly headland soon after to do some filming, the only vegetation that wasn't burnt to a complete crisp was the xanthorrhoea or grass trees that the local Aboriginal people know as *gadi*.

The hardenbergia was named in a distinctly imperial way in honour of Franziska, Countess von Hardenberg, who was a patron of botany and the sister of Baron Von Hugel, who visited Australia in 1833. In 1837 the genus was named after the countess by George Bentham. The distinguished Bentham became president of the Linnean Society, a prestigious role. Bentham was in Vienna around the time he was naming the hardenbergia, and must have been acquainted with Baron Charles von Hugel, who was an esteemed member of Austrian society and a botanist. From November 1833 to October 1834 the baron travelled through Australia and kept a journal, which has been translated by Dymphna Clark and is now in the National Library of Australia.[41] It makes sense that a distinguished English botanist would honour the sister of an esteemed Austrian botanist by naming a genus in the far Antipodes after her. Doesn't it?

I asked one of my artist friends, Rebecca Mayo, what she gleaned about the countess from Dymphna Clark's translation of von Hugel's journal. Off the top of her head, she couldn't recall a single detail of Franziska. She said she'd reread the book and get back to me. A few days later she emailed me. Von Hugel only mentioned her once. In an entry dated 6 October, he notes 'his dear sister Fanny's birthday'.[42] Hmm, she was barely worth a mention? We must make of that what we will.

VIOLENCE AND MURDER

There is a history of human violence towards plants, often due to bioprospecting, over-harvesting and unethical methods of production. Think of how open-cut mines destroy forests and scrub. Think of unsustainable agriculture, where the earth is overworked, eroded and moves beyond the tipping point of replenishment. Think of constant tree-clearing for golf courses, roads and cities that wipes out native trees and underground mycelium systems. Don't forget the legacy of the colonial habit of competitive botanical collecting from far-flung places.

Some might say that the imperialist race to collect plants was just a product of the excitement of the Enlightenment, of acquiring knowledge, of discovering science. Others, that there is always going to be collateral damage with human progress. But history bears witness to the depth of damage.

At first glance, the specimens in the herbarium appear innocent – uprooted from their homes but kept as reminders of lost habitats, information for future botanical science.

In fact, these benign plant specimens are like saviours, with genetic information for a future world. For example, the Sydney herbarium's 1.4 million specimens can be interpreted as rich archives of human interaction with plants, because they record plants from the past and hold genetic information that still can be used for sequencing, propagation and sharing with herbaria around the world. But it's also possible that the beauty and fragility of their seeds, leaves and flowers, and the herbarium's habitat data, mask the hidden stories, some of them violent, of the way they were collected and the associated stories of slavery, of cut-throat methods to collate the best collection and the careless or even deadly extraction of plants from remote places.

Indigenous knowledge is mostly absent in herbaria. This erasure of Aboriginal stories, despite the wealth of species stored on the herbarium's endless shelves, is a kind of cultural violence. There are other violent stories hidden in the herbarium boxes.

The herbarium has historically attracted some attention for violent and even criminal reasons. I met Gordon Guymer, director of the Brisbane herbarium, in 2017. He came across as a mild-mannered botanist, best known for his work as a forensic botanist on a murder case. The case involved Gerard Baden-Clay, who murdered his wife, Allison Baden-Clay, in 2012. He dumped her body under a bridge in the suburb of Brookfield, 14 kilometres from the family home. There were no witnesses and no evidence to determine the killer.

Guymer was called in because there were leaves found in the murdered woman's hair. Guymer identified six species of rainforest myrtle, none of which grew near the bridge where her body was found. However, he went to the Clays' family home and, sure enough, found all six species growing on their property. Guymer explained the prosecution team had to send police out to guard the bridge site so that the defence team couldn't plant any of the six myrtle plants to undermine the case.[43]

Sydney Royal Botanic Garden's Barbara Briggs was called as an expert in a criminal kidnap and murder case back in 1960. Eight-year-old Graeme Thorne was a sweet little Scots College boy who was abducted on his way to school by a man called Stephen Bradley. Graeme's parents had just won the Opera House lottery and their details (name, home address, family members, telephone number) had been published in the newspaper. Six weeks later, Graeme was found dead, his body wrapped in a blanket. Briggs was able to identify plant fragments on the blanket as *Chamaecyparis pisifera* and *Cupressus glabra*. The two trees were found together in a home in Clontarf and this, together with other evidence, led to Bradley's arrest and sentencing to life in prison.

In 399 BCE the Greek philosopher Socrates was accused of corrupting young minds and sentenced to death by *Conium maculatum* – hemlock. He was given a bowl of the prepared hemlock, boiled and steeped so that the dose was high enough to kill him. Hemlock paralyses the respiratory system. It is associated with witchcraft, and Shakespeare, who was reputed to have a substantial medicinal garden, mentions hemlock in *King Lear* and *Macbeth*.[44]

Then there is the violence of the plants themselves. We had a huge hedge of enormous oleander at our old house. This oleander consisted of five large trees that grew in a line and intertwined their branches. They bore pink and white flowers, consecutively. It is a hardy hedge plant and is still grown in Sydney suburbs – it is easy to grow and flowers prettily in spring.

My sons, typically energetic ratbags when they were young, used to play hide and seek in the oleander hedge and break off branches to use as weapons. I was forever warning them not to touch the oleander, which has toxic flowers and leaves. A chewed leaf could kill an adult. I have been asked why I didn't remove the oleander along the boundary fence. I don't have a very good excuse: I simply didn't get around to it. But it's long gone now.

Another poisonous plant, the gympie gympie plant, *Dendrocnide moroides*, which grows in tropical Queensland

and parts of northern New South Wales, wreaks its own violence against humans and animals. It is a rich green tree with heart-shaped horizontal leaves. The stems, fruit and leaves are all covered in fine fur that is actually stinging hairs. Like the cactus, the hairs are small and fine and break off once in the skin, becoming very difficult to remove. The pain can cause swelling (especially around the mouth and eyes) that can end in death or can take months to wear off. Beware the gympie tree.

While it's true there are many other plants that can cause violent death – datura, belladonna – the plant that causes the most violent deaths is tobacco. Friend to many, tobacco's nicotine can be psychoactive and addictive. But the leaves and roots, if eaten, can cause swift death. The question is always about the dose: a small amount is therapeutic, too large a dose can cause death.

While plants have the capacity for violence, it is outweighed by humans' violence towards plants. The research data suggests that the earth's poor biodiversity, its monocultures, its near-extinct remnant habitats, unsustainable agriculture and uncontrollable waste is all a mighty blow to plants.

The herbarium may bear some of the burden of violence, at least in its hidden historical stories. However, its programs of conservation, genetic research, seed-banking, tissue culture propagation and incubation technology work towards sustainable plant futures. Ultimately, it is the human hand that wields violence against plants.

LABYRINTH

Ant plants are epiphyte plants that nestle into the branch-cradles of paperbark trees. They have airy lives, needing no soil and no contact with the earth. They are cousin to the milkweed, which contrarily releases poisonous toxins to drive ants away. The ant plant is interesting as a sustainable plant, and it might teach us some lessons about how to be more sustainable humans. Here again is an example of the herbarium offering information about a plant that may in turn offer solutions for the future.

Ant plants soak up moisture from their friendly paperbark trees (comrades rather than hosts) during the wet season, to last during the dry. Round as a celeriac, the ant plant tubers have a small number of tiny crater-like entry-points around the circumference. The plant is happy to absorb the nutrients from any dead ants or fungi or any detritus such as the remains of prey that the ants bring back to their nest, in return for their shelter. Ants not only tolerate fungi but prefer to live in the ant plant alongside the fungi.[45]

Ant plants are non-parasitic. Ah, to live on fresh air and sunlight! Bulbously tuberous, the ant plants grow to form cavities, where initial tissue has decayed away. These cavities create a complex of tunnels. When you cut open a prickly skinned ant plant, first you have to avoid the biting ants, and then you can see a labyrinth of endless passages, tunnels and rooms.

There are 16 specimen sheets of the ant plant in the herbarium collection. Many were collected during the 1980s in Queensland or Papua New Guinea and two were collected in 1914 from New Britain or 'Ralum, Rabaul, Neu-Pommern, German New Guinea' in Papua New Guinea. New Pommern or New Britain is an island to the east of Papua. After scouring a map, I found the small town of Rabaul on the tip of the north-eastern coast of this smaller island. The truth is that, like Papua New Guinea, the ant plant has multiple colonisers … but in a less destructive way.

Two of the ant plant specimens in the database are illustrative of the tuberous inner workings of the plant – the tunnels and rooms. I'm impressed the botanists were able to open up the tuber and press a piece on the page for safekeeping in the herbarium. On several specimens we can still see the tunnels and holes inside. These examples are bulky enough to require lots of white tape and string to keep them in position on the page.

One particularly odd herbarium specimen has an ant plant with two leaves arcing out of a little root ball. It looks like the golden snitch from *Harry Potter* – the leaves look like wings and the root ball like the desired golden sphere. What I love about the database photograph is that you can zoom in really close and even see the fibres of the white string tying the root ball down. And you can also see all the sinewy knotted roots of the ant plant and even the still-green moss that sticks to those roots. How are they still green? After being in this box since 1914!

In Greek mythology, Daedalus built the first human labyrinth to hide the minotaur. When humans create a labyrinth, the objective is to imprison a metaphorical beast or his slaves. A human labyrinth is a form of dominance because it expresses a will to create a mark, to leave an inscription, or to urge others through a difficult passage towards a certain point. It's a game but it is also an egoistic resolve of mastery.

The fungal partners in the labyrinthine ant plant team have been overlooked.[46] Like many other marginalised communities, the fungi in fact play a critical role due to their diverse abilities. As fungi expert Martin Sheldrake says, 'Fungi are metabolic wizards and can explore, scavenge and salvage ingeniously.'[47] Fungus – like the enslaved, the cheated, the raped, like Ariadne (known as mistress of the labyrinth, who helped save the enslaved from the minotaur) – has learned how to survive in domineering environments.[48] For this reason, they are the perfect teachers in partnership with the ant plant.

Plant, ant and fungi prosper together, snugly supported by the paperbark tree. Can we learn any lessons from this kind of collaboration and minimisation of waste? It seems like the perfect case study for a circular design where the ideal is to have no waste and symbiotic living.

COLLECTING IS A CURSE

There is a thin, sheer membrane between theft and care, especially in the herbarium. What one person thinks of as theft, another considers merely sharing beauty.

My schoolfriend's mother used to pick flowers on her way back from her morning walk each day. A frangipani, a hibiscus, a gardenia. She'd return home with a flower, plucked from someone's garden, tucked behind one ear. One morning I was collecting my friend and her mother came home distressed. A garden owner had yelled at her, called her a thief. She was mortified and deeply offended. I guess I wasn't sure she was innocent or not.

When I needed stuff harvested from nature, I was often given things. My aunty sent down some huge river rocks from her farm for my first garden. A friend sent down some logs recently to put my pots on. So, is that OK? To take from nature, if it's private land? What about collecting shells from the beach? At Gerroa, south of Sydney, there are now signs near the beach warning visitors not to carry away more than 20 shells each.

It wasn't until recently that I started to feel guilty. At One Mile Beach at Port Stephens, I slowly collected about ten beach rocks to start a rockery for my succulent plants. But was I so innocent, as I schlepped each rock up the sand and around the winding hill? I guess I may have cast glances towards the surf lifesavers, in case they saw me, so that suggests a guilty conscience. One Mile is a public beach. So … should I take them back? When does a little become too much?

As I've mentioned, the original *wunderkammer* often had a fake hidden in the collection to send up the ponderously pretentious botanical and zoological elite. The idea was to have a collection of rare and exotic objects from nature, collected from faraway lands. Never mind how ill-gotten these objects may have been. A glass or wooden model of an object was often included in the glass cabinets too. A playful trick.[49] I love the link between real and imagined, or original and fake. However, these wooden or glass versions of natural specimens were also part of a culturally significant process in themselves. Or, at least, they came to be.

The Sydney herbarium's director, Hannah McPherson, showed me some of the wood and glass models of plants in her collection. They were stored at the back of one of the collection rows and there wasn't much light to see the objects as she pulled them from their boxes. But I could see how beautiful they were. Not fakes, actually, but models for education.

There is an interesting history of plant fakes that were educational models. These models became a popular teaching tool in the late nineteenth century. There was an explosion of interest in this kind of knowledge and a German studio called Ziegler began to make plant models. They were intended as three-dimensional models to aid researchers and students and were sent out to all German universities and to 95 other universities and collecting institutions around the world.

The most famous of the modellers in the botanical world are Leopold and Rudolf Blaschka. They were able to create over 4000 models of plants known as the 'glass flowers'. The anatomy and colouring of these models is exceptional.[50] The technical skill is mind-boggling. I wanted to see the database entries for the wood models in the herbarium, which are used by students and researchers to see the plant physiology in three dimensions. But the truth was, while they were there physically, but there wasn't a record for them. They weren't on the database and there weren't any photographs of them. Mysterious.

Real but unreal. Present but flying just under the radar. They are the sorts of objects that you start to wonder if you really saw them. I did see them, and I held them. I turned them over in my hand and worried the box was too heavy for Hannah when she lifted it back up on the shelf. At least … I think I did.

PLANT BLINDNESS

Plant blindness is when humans notice the people and the animals around them, but only think of plants as background. Addressing it is part of my project with the herbarium – to increase awareness of the value of plants, and their conservation and care.

However, I've become aware that some trees *are* noticed and some plants *are* noticed. But not all, and not equally. So plant blindness is a bit selective. I'd go so far as to say the habit of plant blindness is a bit discriminatory.

Take the banksia tree. In the bush, the banksia can be a hero. A goddess. Epically large and full of cones and flowers, throbbing with parrots or wattle birds, they are valorous trees out in the scrub.

But in the cities, they can be a bit ... mangy. That's because they are often separated from their scrubs, the members of their families that help them thrive. There are about 20 banksias in a one-kilometre radius of my house in the city. But they are not heroes or goddesses among trees here. Within this radius, the giant casuarinas are noticeable. They are the ones that whisper to me. Then there are the plane trees that make people sneeze and cough in spring, and whose leaves flicker to cast filmy shadows in the sun.

Probably the most famous trees around me are the jacarandas that explode into purple along the verge outside the Victoria Barracks in Paddington each year. Tourists come and take selfies in front of these mauve eruptions. But no one takes photos in front of the almost-dead-looking banksias. They look abandoned and woody, dried out and brown. Poor banksias. They need a good bit of firestick farming to get their leaves green, their cones open and their branches laden with flowers. Can't do that kind of firing in the city, though.

So plant blindness may only be relevant for the ugly trees. However, I thought I'd ask a few experts what they thought.

I asked three people to let me interview them about plants and record the interviews as videos. A videographer friend with plenty of TV experience did the filming. I invited revered plant scientist Monica Gagliano, who is a dab hand at being interviewed on tape. I also invited Adelaide author Jess White. And my third guest was Graeme Errington, curator at PlantBank at the Australian Botanic Garden at Mount Annan.

My house became a film set for the recording. There were wires, cables, lights and cameras. There was a trolley for one camera to move across. We set up the 'stage' and lined up my favourite pink armchairs, carefully placed all my pot plants behind the scene and even hung some in front of us. The videographer had a pet cockatiel. He brought it with him and before we knew it, that bird was sitting on my shoulder throughout the interviews. I didn't mind at the time but the whole set up and the bird made the final interviews, which are still up on YouTube, look a bit … silly.

Anyway, not having the bandwidth to stop what was happening nor understanding how to do so without compromising the team, we persevered. Monica Gagliano was staying with me and had stowed her sitar upstairs. She always travelled light. Her clothes are usually a cool combo of jeans, favourite worn lace-up boots and a short t-shirt worn over the top of a long sleeved t-shirt.

We interview Monica first because she is a pro. She knows how to communicate her plant science. Her ecology work, her sound work (sonic midwifery) and her plant communication work is all conveyed across peer-reviewed papers, television interviews, conference papers and TED talks. She is hugely popular and well-known and her book, *Thus Spoke the Plant* is a personal narrative of her experience with plants.

Of plant blindness she says, 'Why have we ignored the obvious about plants? Science clearly shows us that plants can do many things. Plant blindness is dangerous because it shows we humans don't care. Science has an important voice and our culture wants validation through science, but some Indigenous knowledge and folklore has been dismissed, belittled and ignored. So there is a lot of catch up to do to avoid future plant blindness and to say that plants know, perceive and behave. So now people can be sure they can pay attention.'

Monica has battled stigma in her plant-science approach. This is because she is experimental and cross-disciplinary in her method – she is both a scientist and a natural narrator. She knows how to gather people together to work. But that doesn't necessarily translate into good support from the university sector. Nevertheless, she has been able to attract millions of dollars of research funding.

Our next interviewee is Jess White. Jess is a researcher in plant studies and has also written about nineteenth-century colonial botanist Georgiana Molloy. Molloy was based in Western Australia and conducted incredible botanical collecting work, despite the difficulties of heat and access, and being a woman. Jess has written what she calls an eco-biography about Molloy. When asked about plant blindness, she drew on her personal experience as a woman who lost most of her hearing when she contracted meningitis as a four year old.

She said, 'The importance of plants and how long they have been on earth is just beyond most humans. It's hard not to anthropomorphise plants, but that is part of the problem. We need to describe plants as something quite different to humans to capture their alienness. They are selves, they are lives. I am a bit ambivalent about the term "plant blindness" because I am quite deaf but that doesn't mean I don't listen. Deaf people are never not listening. So, [we] say someone is blind, without vision, but they do see through braille and in a different way. There is an ableist association with the term plant blindness and we have to remember to look after plants, otherwise we will all die.'

Graeme Errington, our third interviewee, arrived and looked a little astonished at how much stuff was set up for the video. But he was calm and sat and readied himself for my questions.

Before we get onto the subject of plant blindness, Graeme explained the basics of the seed collection at PlantBank, which now sits next door to the new herbarium building at Mount Annan. The PlantBank building has secret rooms for tissue culturing in agar solutions, laboratories all along the corridor with people in lab coats doing botanical research. They have thermo gradient tables, each about a metre square and topped with a large aluminium plate that has a temperature gradient from 5 degrees to 40 degrees so the botanists can put seeds right across that gradient and they can pick up very specific responses to heat.

The herbarium and PlantBank have teams that venture out into the field. In order to maximise the value of the seed material they plan to go and collect, Graeme explains, they need the seeds to be as mature as possible. The maturity of the seed when collected affects how long they can keep it in storage, and it will have an impact on germination as well.

It is at this moment that the cockatiel starts squeaking madly. I urge Graeme on. Of course, the sourcing of seeds is complex.

We think of these expeditions as involving picking up seeds from the ground. But of course it's not that simple. Some seed is held on plants and some seed is dispersed. Graeme reminds us how the banksia has a cone that holds the seed for a number of years until there's a fire, and only then releases the seed. That fire release is called serotiny. Those seeds can be collected over a large amount of time. But other seeds are dispersed as soon as they are mature – the fruit splits and the seeds get dispersed, and so you have to be there at the right time or you miss the opportunity because animals have taken the seed or it's disappeared into the soil.

What Graeme's colleagues at some of the other national seedbanks have found is that there are species that won't germinate at low temperatures, and they won't germinate at high temperatures – they have a very specific envelope when this can happen. Plants become adapted to a certain climate. Some of the Western Australian species that occur on top of a mountain are adapted to a particular temperature range, so what will happen to them given the predicted increases in temperature?

Graeme says, 'One of the things that I, and a lot of my colleagues, have always been very keen on is to get people to understand what we do. It was a bit hard to explain back when we were locked away in the shed up the back of the nursery. But the beautiful thing about PlantBank is that it allows people to come in, and there's interpretation, and they can see what's going on. And then we also have tours where they can get some of the specialists, like myself, to give them behind-the-scenes tours where we can give them the detail of what we do. So, yeah, I think people are always fascinated when they see the range and diversity of what we do.'

And diversity is key here. One of the things that Graeme and the team are doing when they go out to collect is to maximise the capture of genetic diversity, as opposed to an agricultural crop, which is bred to be very uniform in its behaviour, seed storage, growth, harvest and longevity. The PlantBank collections are genetically diverse. There's a whole range of species that come from rainforest communities, for example, that don't have adaptations for dry conditions. They have a different ecological process. A lot of rainforest species tend to germinate immediately and sit as a seedling, so the seed phase is very short for them. So the seeds either don't like being dried, or if they can dry them, they don't like being frozen.

We take a quick break to give Graeme a breather and I'm lured out the back door of my house because I can hear something strange. A thrashing sound. And also an intense meowing. Raised voices. It's two men who live behind my house in a row of townhouses. There is a driveway alongside my house, then a courtyard area and some car parking spaces that back up against the back wall of my garden. The people living in the four townhouses drive in and out past my house. They also drive through a gate that is flanked by two great big mulberry trees. Next to these trees are some banana plants that have grown enormous and some cascading vines that seem to have come from somewhere else and intrepidly escaped to live among us.

Let's just say there's a lot of vegetal action happening just outside my garden wall. But the men are arguing. Man One is a well-groomed older man who is polite and slightly socially detached but not in a bad way. Man Two loves cars. He seems to have lots of them, and these vehicles regularly change.

Man One is cutting bits of the mulberry tree that grows outside the garden wall and drops its fruit into my garden. He is also cutting bits of vine and other shrubs along their communal driveway/car park and throwing everything he cuts over the fence into my backyard. Man Two is trying to stop the cutting. Man One is shouting that he finds it difficult to drive in and out because he can't see the driveway properly through all the greenery. Man Two tells Man One he needs to get a new pair of specs. The greenery is nice, he says, the greenery is part of the charm of the area and why can't Man One see that.

I go out my back gate and go up to the two men. They turn to me.

'Can you please stop doing that?' I ask Man One.

He starts to tell me that it is really none of my business. I put up my hand.

'I mean … Please stop throwing your cuttings over my wall and into my garden.'

Both men turn and peer inside my gate. Man One, who is very angry, has been throwing everything he cuts over my fence, in aggressive lobbing motions. I can tell that he really hadn't even been aware of what he was doing but wanted the greenery that was making him blind, gone. So he muttered a few words and came into my garden and dragged the great pile of branches out. They made a slow, long, scraping sound. A walk of shame.

I shut my gate and headed back inside the house, leaving them arguing. The irony of this disagreement about who or what was causing blindness seemed well timed. Perhaps our interviews could shed some light on the problem.

Graeme and I settle back into our interview chairs. We adjust our clothes and check our hair and the cockatiel flies over to takes up residence on my shoulder. Perhaps that bird could see something in me that I didn't know I had.

I ask Graeme my last question, about plant blindness, and we talk about how there has been some pushback against that term, picking up Jess's comments about ableism.

What it means is the inability of humans to appreciate and acknowledge the plants in their immediate environment. Is PlantBank doing work that might help cure plant blindness?

Graeme replies that there are more than 24 000 plant species in Australia, six and a half thousand of them in New South Wales alone. A lot of people might recognise a gum tree if they saw it, but do they know that there's 700 species of gum? And when it comes to everybody's favourite, the wattle tree, there are approximately a thousand species of those in Australia. So even when people see plants and recognise them, they don't understand the full picture.

People recognise animals, Graeme goes on, because there are fewer of them, so they're easier to remember.

'And they look you in the eye,' I say.

Graeme replies, 'That's one of the reasons why insects get overlooked, and that's where a lot of diversity is.'

But if there were perhaps 200 species of koalas, then people might have a bit of difficulty understanding that as well. One of the things the botanic garden is really focused on is getting people to understand diversity. In an urban environment, even if people see trees, Graeme says, they don't necessarily understand what those trees give them. They might when it's a really hot day and they're standing in the shade of one. But the other things that trees are constantly doing, providing a habitat for birds and animals, filtering pollution, ameliorating the local extremes of temperature – these things, which trees just do sitting in the background, make our life pleasant.

I know Graeme's sentiments are shared at the gardens and among the PlantBank staff. It would be hard to argue against how important plants are.

But as I listen to Graeme I wonder what the plants think about all this busy work in our botanical institutions. The thermo thing. The cryo place. The tissue stuff. It's science and it is anticipating the future. It is highly attractive work. No doubt. I just wish we knew if it was the right method, the right approach, the most efficient way towards biodiversity.

Later as I wave goodbye to the interviewees, I gaze out from my porch and see the tips of some ugly banksias jutting up beside a row of houses.

I know we haven't solved any problems for those banksia trees. These urban versions of themselves are never going to be heroes in the city streets while they are disconnected from their kinship scrub. It seems a little bit sad. There has to be a way to reclaim those goddesses in waiting. Maybe I'll walk round later and give them a haircut and throw down some organic fertiliser.

CATHY OFFORD
AND THE WOLLEMI

People get *very* excited about the Wollemi pines – or, as some people call them, the dinosaur trees. They are huge. They are old. They are knowing. And their location is a secret, for conservation reasons.

It's the idea of these ancient trees being hidden from the colonial eye in a secret, protected location that attracts interest. It's also the fact that, according to fossil research, they are as old as 200 million years. The Wollemi, which was discovered after being thought extinct, is a story of care and conservation and also of the critical importance of sometimes not revealing information that might adversely affect the trees. The extreme measures undertaken to protect these secret pines during the 2019–2020 bushfires add another element to the story that is important to hear.

The story begins in 1994, when an off-duty National Parks and Wildlife ranger and experienced canyoner called David Noble was trekking in remote bush in the Blue Mountains west of Sydney and found trees that had only been known through their fossils. Wollemi pines are huge trees that can grow over 40 metres high with trunks more than a metre in diameter. They have two ranks of pine-like leaves, like tough fronds, along their branches and droop a bit. The bark looks like the bubble-rock skin of the character Thing in the film *The Fantastic Four* – that is, like very dry and cracked desert land.

One interesting point to note is that these secret trees were named *Wollemia nobilis* soon after 1994, to honour David Noble who discovered them. The tree also has the Aboriginal name of Wollemi, which was chosen as that is the place the trees were found. The pine trees grow in ledges of watery rock in a deep gorge and almost no one knows the location.

One woman who knows the location is Cathy Offord, senior scientist at the Royal Botanic Garden, Sydney. She explains that the groves of Wollemi are at risk and need to be protected. You can see Wollemi trees growing in in many botanic gardens around the world, including in Sydney, Mount Annan and Mount Tomah. Seeing a younger Wollemi at a nursery or germinating in a botanic garden might make people think the call for conservation and keeping the location secret is a bit silly, but the new trees are not the same as the mega old ones. The dinosaur trees have massive root networks and are the grand dames of their environment.

People sometimes don't understand why it's important to keep big old trees in the ground. *Just plant new ones*, people say. *Stop making such a fuss.* But we need to make a fuss. It's hard to decide if humans or the increasing number and scale of bushfires are more of a threat to the Wollemi. It's the cumulative effect of bushfires that drives plant extinctions. In other words, one bushfire that reaches the canopy and burns everything out is bad, but the plants and trees will remain resilient and regrow. However, when there are constant similar bushfires, it gets harder for the bush to recover.

Cathy Offord explains that the wild Wollemi pines did get burnt during the 2019–2020 fires, but it wasn't too devastating because of 'the huge efforts of our team and we were able to mitigate against complete annihilation'. So as word of the bushfires got underway, the recovery team acted on a plan for catastrophic fire that had been in place for many years.

Cathy and her team connected for many meetings to work out a strategy to minimise damage to the trees. They were water-bombing along ridge lines and laying down retardant and assessing the risks. The retardant chemical is bad for plants, fauna and soil, and this had to be weighed against how bad the effects of a full-force fire hitting the trees could be. They decided to put down the retardant at quite a distance from the trees, but in such a way that would stop the progress of fire.

The fire-fighting team did more than organise fire retardant and water-bombing. They also abseiled down into the gorge and put in irrigation around the Wollemi plants from the creek to keep them moist. Cathy says, 'There is footage of the fire going through. It singed a lot of the Wollemi trees and some were badly burnt and some unaffected. It shows us that as Australia is getting drier there are more fires and higher frequency of fires. If plants and trees like these are getting burnt every 50 years then it will be death by a thousand cuts.'

Cathy adds that the 1994 fire in the Blue Mountains National Park was a bad one, then a few years later more frequent fire events started to happen. This, she explains, is what leads to extinctions. Some species are stimulated by fire. People see trees regrowing after the fires but those green shoots are signalling that the trees are trying to recover and they are expending a lot of energy to do that. And after fire, there is an abundance of weeds competing with native species to establish themselves. Anything less than 15 years between fires will negatively affect plants.

I search through the database that the herbarium's Hannah McPherson has given me, and scroll down to the Wollemi trees. I wondered if the herbarium database would be as intriguing as the real stories of the Wollemi trees. It does not disappoint. There are 41 entries in the database. *Wollemia nobilis* from the araucariaceae family. Some of the entries merely say 'site 4' under the locality field in the database. Under 'county', the entries are mostly 'the Central Tablelands'. Covering over 30000 square kilometres from Oberon to Mudgee, this location is vague enough. The vast majority of records note that the 'precise locality and lat/long [latitude and longitude] omitted'. That's reassuring.

There are two specimens stored in the spirit collection, which means they are too bulky to have been pressed onto the page. Other descriptions note cones and fruit. Some were cultivated at Mount Annan. There's a note on one specimen that its leaves had been sent to a scholar at Southern Cross University for a phytolith study (phytolith is the tiny rigid stone-like silica inside plant tissue).

I love all this hidden scientific information about the secret Wollemis, but there is only one problem. For some reason, there are only two images available on the database. It is a shame, and a mystery, that there are only two images. But they are beauties. One is a specimen taken from a cultivated Wollemi at Mount Annan, noting its original wild source was Wollemi National Park. Its tapered leaves are neat as a hacksaw. They seem to branch out in spurts, tapering back in and then spurting out again. More like a hacksaw that can't make up its mind.

The second specimen sheet is like the most perfect specimen sheet ever invented. It has a bright colour chart (like your average eyeshadow palette) to the side. It also has a black-and-white centimetre ruler chart to the side for scale. There are three small branches, one with a tiny cone forming at its tip. It is a holotype – a type specimen upon which the description and name of the new species is based. In other words, this is an important specimen sheet.

The notes on the sheet also say that the specimen, which is now browned but in crisp and clear condition, was taken from a small stand of coachwood forest in a deep sheltered sandstone gorge. This sheet does actually give the general latitude and longitude of the tree's location. But I won't share the secret location, obviously, because I (like the botanic gardens team) want these grand trees to survive.

THE PLANT ARTISTS

Picture an artist living in New Mexico. She lives in a mud house. By day, she can often be found sitting in her rocking chair, waiting for inspiration to rumble across the deserts. But she has to be ready to catch the idea. Once it is within reach, she then paints large canvases using a ruler and pencil to grid out meditative patterns that create an optical experience that verges on spiritual exultation.

Painting after painting, an endless practice of mindfulness. The artist was Canadian–American artist Agnes Martin (1912–2004). When I was 21 and living in New York doing an internship at the Metropolitan Museum of Art for my Masters degree, I saw an exhibition of Agnes Martin's paintings at the Pace Gallery. It was the winter of 1991–1992.

That exhibition of paintings taught me that art could change my outlook on everything. Alter my state of mind. Enhance my perception. I stumbled out of the exhibition feeling like the only thing worth knowing was an artist's version of the world. I also knew it would be my job to share artists' stories, over and over again.

Art has the capacity to change viewers and it also has the ability to mediate tough ideas. Art that incorporates plant life has a different kind of power. It draws attention to how precious plants are and exposes some of the damage humans have done to the environment. It also celebrates new relationships with plants.

As part of our research project with the herbarium, my colleague Marie Sierra at the University of Melbourne chose four artists to respond to the specimens in the herbarium collection. They were selected from a much larger field. So on a lucky day, the artists and I went down to the new herbarium at Mount Annan to see what was what. We expected to only view it from the outside but were pleasantly surprised.

The herbarium building had just been completed. The walls are rammed earth. Rammed earth is a process of building formwork and then shovelling in layers and layers of gravel and sand – sometimes yellow, sometimes creamy pink – and then pressing down each layer, and repeating, so that each layer is visible in the final wall. Like a multi-layered sponge cake.

Rammed earth has the effect of making a new sandy wall look ancient, pebbly and touchable. The herbarium has six huge vaults with curved fronts. The vaults are also made of rammed earth with soaring tin roofs. Each vault houses a genus of plants.

The day we visited, we had no idea we would be able to get a sneak peek inside the building as it hadn't opened to the public. Nor had all the specimens been moved into the new space yet. The plant-move was complicated. There were 1.4 million specimens to be photographed, packed up, trucked from the Domain to Mount Annan and then put in a freezer for a week, outside the herbarium. Once the plants had been frozen for a week, they were brought inside the building and left to acclimatise for a few days before being packed away into their new rolling cupboards.

Artists Fabri Blacklock and Anna Raupach and I arrived at PlantBank, adjacent to the new herbarium. This was before Anna had her interaction with Joel Cohen about access to the herbarium's database for her app. We were loitering a little. You know, peering in through windows and doors and wandering around aimlessly. There was a lot of chatting among us about the herbarium collection and how Fabri was going to dye fabrics, and Anna was going to create an augmented reality phone app with sound and visuals that responded to GPS locations of trees. This exciting work was all in response to the collection of plant specimens.

I was taking some photos for a fourth artist who was also going to be installing artwork within a few months and hadn't been able to make it to meet us. John Siemon, the director of PlantBank, saw us milling about and unlocked the PlantBank doors and let us in. Shortly after, the operations manager took us through the new herbarium building too.

It's kind of spooky to walk around a building that hasn't been used before. Everything was ready. There were phones hooked up. New chairs at every table. Even the tea room had appliances plugged in and the fridge humming. Hard to explain why a new building makes you feel uneasy. Maybe it was too clean. The windows had no smudges, the walls had no scuff marks. I guess it is because the before-shot looks a bit like the apocalyptic after-shot.

We set off down a long corridor, our footsteps echoing as we wandered down and looked in on each vault's vestibule where researchers could sit at desks and conduct their work. Inside each of the six massive vaults was a wall of rolling cupboards, a compactus like those in library stacks. I started to imagine what the space would be like once it was full of life, full of plants. There would be folders everywhere and probably microscopes and reference books.

The artists started quietly joking about getting squashed between the herbarium's stacks, and how to quickly throw yourself out of them before someone turned the handle of the stack shelf and squashed you senseless.

Again, I think the light-heartedness had something

to do with being in a place we weren't really supposed to be. The operations manager had permission to show us the entrance but she had ended up taking us all the way through the vaults. Lotte Van Richter, we thank you. Lotte explained that the temperature in the massive building was helped by the cool air flow between the rooms and the floating tin roof. Each vestibule reported 16 degrees Celsius and 44 per cent humidity. The drying room for incoming seeds is 15 per cent humidity, so 44 per cent struck me as quite high, but I suppose if the plants get too dry they might snap off with handling.

Fabri is a woman with a formidable capacity to make art and to generate important Australian Indigenous projects. She and Anna were to be the first two artists to respond to the plants in the collection. The art component of our herbarium project was called Tellus and was funded by the Australian Research Council. The following year, artists Erica Seccombe and Rebecca Mayo would interpret the collection too, but in completely different ways.

Fabri's family are Nucoorilma/Ngarabal people from Tingha and Glen Innes and Biripi people from Dingo Creek in New South Wales. She is also a textiles artist with an intense work ethic, and at the time was juggling our exhibition and another major deep-listening and yarning project with multiple female Elders right across New South Wales. Fabri is also a colleague of mine at the University of NSW's School of Art and Design, so I have seen firsthand how hard she works to improve education equity for Aboriginal and Torres Strait Islander peoples and how quick she is to support people who enter the system as students or lecturers.

Fabri had come to Mount Annan with her son and a family friend, Aunty Zona Wilkinson, who is a Gamilaroi Elder from Mount Druitt. Aunty Zona has a rich background of working as an artist (ceramics and painting), as a curator and community leader. She walked with purpose and the confidence of a strong, proud and respected Aboriginal woman.

As Fabri, Aunty Zona, the herbarium operations manager and I walked around the interior of PlantBank to sort out how the artworks would be hung, the sound quality for Fabri's oral history recordings and video projections, I could see Aunty Zona was itching to say something. Eventually she said, 'I'd like to know something.' We all turned to her. 'Are there any bush tucker gardens here?'

In fact the Mount Annan botanic garden has a strong connection with the local Aboriginal community and has constant Indigenous programs, but they are sometimes hard to see because they are embedded in education programs. While Sydney's Royal Botanic Garden does have an Aboriginal Strategy Officer, there is probably more work than one person can cover. Mount Annan also has strong alliances with the Campbelltown Local Aboriginal Land Council and the Campbelltown Arts Centre. There is also the moving Dharawal Stolen Generation memorial in the old Cumberland remnant bush. But Aunty Zona has a point: where are the other permanent Indigenous knowledge fixtures or points? Where is the Indigenous bush tucker garden?

What I'm drawn to about Aunty Zona is that her expression is both calm and fierce, polite but firmly challenging. Even better is the way Fabri roars with laughter when Aunty Zona asks her probing questions.

After that day, Aunty Zona and Fabri go on to dye the most exquisite silks using eucalyptus leaves, boiling them up in a huge pot. Later, they hang from the concrete walls of PlantBank and draw attention to the beauty of nature without detracting from the science that is undertaken in the buildings.

That is the real test of plant-centred art. To make aesthetic objects of beauty that don't compete with the natural world, but instead raise awareness of how precious it is. Our project included artists, writers and film-makers. They all responded to the call of particular plants. Perhaps the biggest surprise was the poets we commissioned to revalue the plants in the collection. The poets managed to decolonise the plant collection, revere the plants and evoke a sense of awe.

Art is an emotional memory of the world. Art is an emotional memory of Australia's history. Without Indigenous art, Australia's memory is not complete. I've spent many years writing about art for journals and books, papers and magazines. It's not easy to communicate feeling, or affect, because it's so individual. But art and poetry have the capacity to raise us up, to make us listen a bit more closely and to look a little more carefully. It also has the effect of opening up the world for a while. As Fabri's silk hangings move slightly in the corridors of PlantBank, they make me think of the tens of thousands of years that Aboriginal and Torres Strait Islander people have been working with the eucalyptus tree.

The second thing about art and poetry that is relevant to the herbarium is how these cultural and artistic practices mirror natural environments. Art mimics nature which mimics art which mimics nature which mimics art. It's a never-ending gyre of continuous culture and Western humanity's biggest mistake has been to glibly pretend that art and nature are discrete and separate. If we whitefellas have learned anything from Indigenous people, it is that everything is connected.

DAKOTA AND THE FLAME TREE POEM

On a steep ridge below an old forest at Mount Annan, there was a new planting happening and poetry was being recited.

Here, along with the remnant Cumberland Plain Woodland of grey box, eucalyptus, forest red gum, ironbark and stringybark trees that once covered 120 000 hectares of the western Sydney area, there are also cabbage gums, angophoras and broad-leaved apple trees.

There is something expansive about Mount Annan, which is a contrast to the meticulously cultivated botanic gardens at the Domain. When you drive in through the gates at Mount Annan, there are hills of native grasses: it's dry and the soil is clay. Mount Annan smells of the bush – dry, consistent and menthol, twiggy, with the hot taste of grasses at the back of your throat. Whereas the city botanic garden smells of plants – exotic, wet, multiple, a competing diversity of aromas … more floral.

But on this day, there was a particular group gathered. The atmosphere was calm and people were dotted all up and down a slope that had been recently cleared of African olive trees. So the hill was bare of trees and the soil had been turned over. A cluster of people were preparing for a smoking ceremony.

More people wandered over and chatted in groups. There was no structure to the occasion as yet. Everyone was milling, waiting. There were botanic garden staff in their khaki uniforms, looking plant-knowledgeable and capable. Then a minibus full of Indigenous Elders chugged its way across the grass from the road. They piled out and wandered over to the slope too. Then a group of kindergarteners from a local school arrived in their sunhats with those legionnaire flaps at the back to protect their necks from the sun. Super cute.

This was a Poem Forest event, organised by the amazing Tamryn Bennett of Red Room Poetry. We were going to plant native trees all up and down the slope and there were gloves and trowels for everyone to use. Word spread through the patches of people about what to do and slowly people began to bend and plant, bend and plant. Uncle Ivan Wellington, a Yuin Elder who I'd met on that sunny day at the Campbelltown Art Centre, gave a Welcome to Country and then conducted a Smoking Ceremony. The wind picked up the ceremonial smoke and was easy to share among the group.

We learned that there was some remnant forest on the very top ridge of the hill – behind a line of the African olive trees – and Uncle Ivan remembered playing there when he was younger and the olive trees hadn't yet taken over the site.

Everyone moved in close to listen respectfully as Uncle Ivan started to speak about his childhood. There were generations of pain in his stories that needed to be heard. The director of the Royal Botanic Garden and the director of Mount Annan were there to listen deeply, and other community members who understood his experiences.

Once the speeches were done, the trees were planted and the poetry read, the group disassembled and floated away from the slope followed by some traces of the eucalyptus smoke. I fell in step with one of the poets who had recited his poem. Dakota was easy to chat to, same age as my sons, and open as twenty-somethings are. His story was an articulate explanation of his studies, his future plans, his love of poetry. In a word: impressive, but with a hint of sadness.

I left the event, feeling sated. Cleansed by the smoke. Comforted by the sombre but thoughtful energy of the day. About six months later, I emailed Dakota Feirer, a Bundjalung–Gumbayngirr man, and asked him to write a poem for our herbarium project. He chose the flame tree.

The flame tree has straight trunks and branches that often seem to come off the middle trunk rather than branching from branches. They have three-pronged green leaves that drop in November, replaced by blooms of red – like deflated balloons of bright colour. In Sydney, the flowering of the great jacarandas often overshadows the flames, but they flower together and are often planted together. The flame tree is the less popular sibling.

While Dakota and I were tossing ideas back and forth about the flame tree, he explained the concept of a yarn to me. An Indigenous yarn, Dakota explained, is a noun and a verb. You enact it, perform it. He gives an example of the word in a sentence: 'Have you got that yarn?' No one owns a yarn, he says, and it's both static and fluid. You can come back to a yarn and there might be new meaning. Yarns are connected to bigger yarns.

But Dakota adds to this traditional story of a yarn by saying 'Narrative contains us, narrative is a universal marker of existence.' White history is a big, wrong story. New knowledge is reorganised into story. Whereas individual stories move away from connection and land. This is tricky for me to understand because I'm used to single stories. One person telling a story. Well ... that's not completely true. There are those family stories where everyone is shouting over the top of each other. But that is not an Indigenous yarn.

What Dakota loves about the flame tree is that 'it's different each year, in each location, but it's connected to its place and has a reason for being there as an ecosystem for birds and its deeper connection with the earth and water. The flame tree is sentient and has intelligence it has a feminine power'.

Later I found a feather on the ground. Multicoloured. Probably a green parrot. I took it home and put it in my cabinet of curiosity. These months later, writing about the flame tree, I have it next to me on the desk. In each hair of the feather more stories seem to glisten. About flight. About cold air. About shaving close to tree canopies. I wish I were a bird.

`Brachychiton acerifolius` `by Dakota Feirer`

habitNotes
'A red flowering Kurrajong. Sergeant Clark writes:
– seeds from this tree have been sown on many occasions but
… there from invariably produces a white flower.'

recordedBy
Bloodstained pages frame
rules of
an imperial game
embroidered
emboldened
embellished
executioners, knighted by
'ologists
precious appellatives

family
Each stroke
of ink
on paper
equals
imperial
salutation
deepening
scars
on sacred land and paperbarks.

habitat
Though true
depth is absent
from inkpot.
Buoying
a royal
crown
above the deepest
ocean
of stories.

genus
Deified
authorities
waltzing matilda
through their
curated gardens

of stolen knowledge
falsehoods
dancing above
a terra nullius.

scientificName
Botany has
both raped and erased
your flame
stifled
your
beauty
POISON
marks
your name now.

specificEpithet
Under the guise
of a blind Latin
tongue
seeds and leaves
crushed between leather
of boot and journal
now mere shadows
pressed
across spreadsheet.

notes

songlines are no less dismembered beyond these cells
roots thread deeper than introduced infrastructure
when belly holds water and hands bleed rivers
holding memory and babies. women's business tree.

About six months after Dakota wrote this poem for *The Herbarium Tales* (the website which records all the outputs from our research project collaboration with the herbarium), there was the chance to take the poem to Edinburgh Festival. AIATSIS, the Australian Institute of Aboriginal and Torres Strait Islander Studies, offered to fund a video of Dakota speaking his poem to camera (along with two other poets) so that it could be shown to a Scottish and international audience.

Dakota directed his own performance as he recited his poem. Most of the filming is within an archival space. Then towards the end, he takes off his shoes and socks and disappears down a building's lift. When he emerges on the ground floor, he is carrying a protest sign and he joins an activist march in the city. It's a march for women's rights, for choice around the issue of birth control and the right to have an abortion. Dakota joins this march in solidarity. It becomes a pure evocation of the last part of his poem – a tribute to human rights. The flame tree is a women's business tree.

Women's business is women's business. Don't forget it.

THE PLANT SMELLS
OF MEMORY

My first plant love was the lantana, so it's all her fault. That woody and impenetrable scrubby plant that snags clothes and scratches shins, also has lovely pink, yellow and orange flower petals. Its allure often obscures hidden danger beneath or within it. Growing up, we had a lantana hedge high above a retaining wall. Behind the hedge, lawn sloped up to the house on a steep hill.

One day, hiding in my secret space among the lantana with its fog of butterfly acolytes flapping around me, I crawled deeper into the hedge. From this position, I could see people walking along the street or driving by. This was Sydney in the late 1970s and there wasn't much action, to be honest, but eventually I'd see a neighbour yelling at his wife or a cheeky dog escaping its owners as they tried to grab it. Sydney summers were endless and throbbed with warm boredom.

The lantana, despised by some as an invasive weed, loved by others for attracting coastal wrens, had a different story in mind. On this day southerly storm clouds moved in as I was hiding in its branches and an odd thing started to happen: I thought I could hear the plant. Talking. To me. Not in a friendly 'secret lives of plants' kind of juju way. This was more of a scratchy, multi-voiced way. Even at eight years old, I knew I was imagining things. I was young but not stupid and so assumed it was just the wind making the branches scrape together. I also assumed the high-pitched squealing sound that combined with the scraping sound was the leaves being tossed around by the sudden gusts of cooler air.

It was illogical but the noises seemed to escalate. I instinctively knew that the plant was not trying to reveal something to me. It just wanted me *out*. I heeded this strange message and I moved backwards (on my knees and crouched over) through the thick hedge, not caring that my arms were being scratched. Feeling like the lantana was ejecting me more and more with each minute, I moved my knee back one more time, lost my balance and fell the three metres to the footpath below. I broke my wrist. My mother had to cancel her dinner party (she had all the Marimekko dinner plates out) and take me to the hospital. I never played in the lantana again. But that plant still grows along Sydney's coastal cliffs and it still connects with me. I always grab one of its flowers and watch the colours swim together as I twirl the petals.

Plants intrigue. Plants challenge. Sometimes plants even shame us. But they also trigger memories. It's nice to walk on the bed of overlapping scale-like leaves that have fallen beneath a Norfolk Island Pine, leaves that are more like little spiky swords than conventional leaves. But even better than the soft mound of fallen swords is the smell. That fresh, woody, slightly citrus smell is sometimes associated with floor cleaner. But for me, it conjures my childhood holidays at a beach north of Sydney. So that woody, fresh smell brings up really clear images of cricket on the beach, the pink of sunsets on the sand, the taste of ocean foam at the back of your throat when it rushes up your nose and the feeling of sandy grit in your cozzie. Summer. Salty air. Sunburn.

Maybe everyone has a lantana story – a tale where the plants take over, conquer us, or fail to seed, refuse to thrive, or poison us. The more time spent with plants, the more it becomes clear that plants are in control and humans are under the false impression that plants need us to survive. This is an interesting conundrum because in our gardens the evidence suggests the latter is true: if we don't water our houseplants, they die. If we don't grow our tomatoes in full sun, they die. All this is true. But these examples (and any others you could possibly come up with) are about how plants need us so that they can help us. So plants need us, but only if we expect them to feed us, shade us or provide medicine. Us. Us, Us.

Cacti expert Liam Engel thinks that plants have colonised us, rather than the reverse. I think I know what he means. Humans grow crops, harvest and sell them. Agriculture is part of what we know. Humans plant flowers and hedges. They create vegetal sanctuaries and tend them with care. We know this too. While we need to remember that plants would still grow even if there are no humans left on earth, it is still beneficial to have good human–plant symbioses.

There are people in positions of authority in these human–plant relations. Who decides what research is done? Who decides which plants are to be publicly grown? What is horticultural best practice?

John Siemon, the Royal Botanic Garden's director of horticulture, is one of the humans in charge of the plants. He was responsible for PlantBank's exquisite seedbank and tissue culture building out at Mount Annan.

Like me, John remembers plants through smell, and in certain instances through his lack of smell or 'anosmia'. He grew up in the leafy suburbs of Brisbane, but his mother loved English country gardens. In their subtropical environment, she managed to grow daffodils, tulips, poppies, bluebells and sweet peas quite successfully. Sweet peas smell a little like roses but with a hint of orange.

'For me it's all about not just visual senses but also smell,' says John. 'So, I can't walk past sweet peas and not smell them. It's a very distinctive scent and it takes you right back. Plants do that in many ways – it might be a taste, a scent and texture, an appearance.'

John explains that there was a cultural shift when staff moved into the state-of-the-art PlantBank. Originally they all worked out of tin sheds and then, once they moved into the fishbowl of the new building (the labs are glassed and the public can peer in to watch the botanists at work), he wondered whether the staff might sneak away from these very public areas to do their work.

However, he says, in fact they are proud to show the public what work is being done, and demonstrating what PlantBank does to help make science relevant. John is right when he describes the feeling of PlantBank as being like the TV series *CSI*. The glamour of the lab, the excitement of forensic testing, is evident at PlantBank. Rather than catching a killer, however, they are finding ways to save endangered plants and address rising temperatures and more frequent fires.

'We are in a great position to conserve plants at Plant-Bank,' he says. 'I'm thankful for every resource around us.' Now, as director of horticulture, he is responsible for managing almost 750 hectares of public green space across three botanic gardens – at Mount Annan, Mount Tomah in the Blue Mountains and the Domain – and more than 17 000 species of plants from across the globe.

As John goes on to speak about his background and what he describes as his 'plant nerdiness', he mentions something about incubators. My ears prick up. Exactly what are the plant incubators? John explains that the incubators can recreate the seasons of spring–summer–autumn–winter for plants.

If there is a new species that hasn't been grown before (often plants coming into the building are new to Western science and new to propagation and conservation), the staff can drop seeds into each of four seasons to see which cues work well. Temperature and light are obviously key settings. Out in the environment it's more complicated to recreate the various conditions because there is no control. But in a bank, you can put the seeds in a petri dish with agar and this gives moisture, support and water for the seed to germinate.

Light is either on or off for the incubators. Typically, many species will germinate at a temperature of around 21 degrees Celsius. But alpine species need stratification, so it has to be really cold, below zero and perhaps 4 degrees for two weeks to mimic germination. Others might need a really hot period and some might need fire. Some need friends, like mycorrhiza (fungi), such as orchids. Orchid seeds need fungus and the mycelium breaks down leaves and transfers nutrient to seeds. Otherwise nothing will happen. Then there is the fire and the banksia.

I ask if this is serotiny – where some species need fire or smoke for seeds to be released and germinated. John nods. 'Yep, we light up a banksia cone as it sits on metal sheet. We flame it with a blowtorch ...'

The fire does three things – in the case of banksias, it causes the seed follicles to open up; it causes the acacias (wattles) to crack their seed coats; and the smoke penetrates into the soil and the carbon layer, post-bushfire, is critical for new growth. When rain hits the burnt chemicals, it gets absorbed into the soil and the tree.

The other germination process, John explains, is when the seed passes through a bird's digestive tract. A few years ago, Cathy Offord and her team at the Royal Botanic Garden simulated this germination process. They fed persoonia seeds to emus at an emu farm. Emus stored the seed in their crop (which is like a gullet) because the seeds are like pebbles. Cath's team collected the emu poo and processed the seeds to see whether they grew better.

Persoonia are interesting because there is the embryo, its surrounding tissue and the seed coat. The normal germination process converts starch to sugar and ultimately triggers the shoots and roots to grow. Persoonia don't have endosperm (the starchy tissue) so they are hard to germinate in a lab or nursery. Hard science to trick.

I ask about sound. The scientists can recreate temperature and light and rainfall, they can even mimic fire. But what about the acoustics of new growth?

John laughs. 'You'll have to ask Brett Summerell about that. Brett thinks the idea of playing music to help plants grow is a bit hokey. We are sceptics, Brett and I. Most scientists are, but we are always happy to be proved wrong.'

The PlantBank building is bushfire resistant and it works as a research facility and a public engagement building. There are freezer rooms, microscopy labs, tissue culture rooms; the CSI-style blue light and lab equipment being used every day is visible to the public. There are exquisite interpretation panels with histories and futures.

The PlantBank building will one day hold 25 000 seed-bearing plant species and, if properly stored, can grow each viable seed that any scientist wishes to study for any application.

'The investment is worth it,' John says. 'The building can do an awful lot, we really don't appreciate the true value of every seed – food, drink, clothes, medicine and alcohol. Plants are so important but it's always the animal with eyelashes that attracts the dollars, rather than plants.'

I question this, because I feel there has been a shift in valuing plants over the last four to five years. This is in part because of a growing academic interest in plant studies but also what seems to be a renewed interest in gardening at any size.

'Yes,' says John. 'There has definitely been shift in perception of plants, after the 2019–2020 bushfires, and after Covid. There is new behaviour towards outdoor places and plants. During Covid, every nursery was sold out and stripped of seed stock.'

Smells are important for humans. Can plants smell? Back in the 1980s, Sydneysiders were able to burn off their waste. My family had an incinerator right next to our hills hoist. This was a common coupling in the suburbs of Sydney back then. My dad would stoke the fire and burn off any cardboard or rubbish, food scraps and even bits of old cloth on occasion. The smell of the wood he would start with was comforting and familiar. We had a Greek family next door and the incinerator was right next to one of their back bedroom windows.

Our Greek neighbours never complained about our incinerator because they had one too.

It's only now, looking back, that I notice something. I am honestly shocked that it never occurred to me before. Because our incinerator, tended to with such everyday pride, was located in the far corner of the back garden, it was very close to three adjoining properties. We had the Greek family behind, the Jewish family next door, and at the diagonal point lived my friends the South Africans. The daughter of that family is still one of my closest friends 45 years later.

The reason I bring up the incinerator is that on our South African friends' land, only a metre or so away from our burning waste, was a middle-sized banksia tree. It was not as beautiful as the angophora on our side but it was a very healthy tree. The neighbour's banksia was at the furthest point of their garden, away from their house, and it shielded them from the smoke of our incinerator and also provided privacy between the two properties.

It's only now that I realise our incinerator smoke was probably the reason that banksia tree was thriving. Banksias need smoke to open their cones and release seeds. It is critical for their health and for maintaining their evolutionary traits. But do they also smell the smoke? They release volatile organic compounds that can be identified by other plants. Although plants do not have noses, they can experience aromas. They can respond to that olfactory-like activity – which helps to deter insects, attract bees and react to diseases close by.[51]

But banksia trees smell like almonds when they burn. I know this from when I visited North Head immediately after the 2020 bushfire, as the ground was still smouldering.

Finally, back to John Siemon and his sweet pea. I ask him how he would describe the aroma of a sweet pea.

'Sweet and musky,' he says. John hasn't smelled sweet peas for a couple of years, but his childhood connection with them is still intense. Like me with pine needles and beach cricket, John recalls memories of riding along on his rollerblades and flying into a bed of canna lilies, and riding his tricycle off his Brisbane balcony, landing in rose bushes and the thorns poking into him. Typical boy, I think, remembering my own sons' kamikaze activities on anything that moved.

And in a strange twist, he shares the fact that there are some flowers he can't smell. They are the native flowers, boronia. There may be other species he can't smell as part of this genetic 'defect' but this is the flower he knows of.

As I look at John's still-boyish features, I suspect he will grow some sweet peas, now that we have talked about them. No doubt he is grateful for the flowers he *can* smell. I'll ask him next time we meet.

THE RIGHTS OF PLANTS

The rivers in New Zealand are icy cold, even in summer. If you are brave enough to strip off and get submerged, it steals the breath from you. After a river swim – for me it's never more than a dunking – I tend to need a haggard, gasping breath as I climb out.

That feeling of extreme cold makes your legs a bit wobbly as you try to get the hell out, staggering over the smooth grey stones and rushing water to the bank. Something else happens, though. You have a feeling of extreme well-being for hours and days afterwards. It clears your head. I mean it literally slows the blood at your temples. That sense of knocking your socks off is addictive.

The Whanganui River is one of these icy rivers. It is chilled by melted snow falling from the high mountain peaks in waterfalls and rivulets. There are both deep currents and rushing water along the river, which starts at Tongariro and flows 260 kilometres to the Tasman Sea.

In 2015 the New Zealand government established the Whanganui River ecological region as a legal entity – essentially legal personhood – so that the river can be represented in a court of law if it is damaged in any way by human hands. Damage to the river is still a threat from farms and forestry developments along its length, potentially causing runoffs of fertiliser and waste that could impact the river's health.

In 2019 two people were selected to speak on behalf of the river: Dame Tariana Turia, an influential Māori political leader, and Turama Hawira, an experienced Māori advisor and educator. The river's personhood is part of earth jurisprudence, where the concepts of law are applied to the earth. The *Te Awa Tupua Act 2017* granting the Whanganui River system legal personhood refers to the Māori reverence for the river as ancestor or *tupuna*.

It's an area of legal study that is starting to make ripples in legislative practice around the world. Unfortunately, these principles are not being represented in Australian courtrooms nor being discussed around the policy-making tables of our parliament.

This change to the protection of ecologies is a new legal representation for plants. There have been unofficial efforts to protect natural entities, such as Buddhist ordainments of trees, but these are tricky processes to refine and harness, or have supported by courts of law. There have been some legislative successes so far, such as the Swiss and Ecuadorian legislation amendments in 2008. A clause was added to legislation to establish the rights of nature in both cases. The International Rights of Nature Tribunal, held in Ecuador 2014 and Peru in 2014 and Paris in 2015, are all documented by the Global Alliance for the Rights of Nature. Declarations and proposals are starting to proliferate, including from the International Union for the Conservation of Nature, whose members are working to protect the rights of ecologies and individual areas.

The aim of these bodies is to move towards a Universal Declaration for the Rights of Nature. But there are a few issues. How do we protect some ecologies and not others? If we protect an old fig tree in Sydney, should we protect all the other fig trees as well? Can we protect lantana, a pretty weed with its colourful little pink, yellow and purple flowers, and not mosses or lichen? Can we protect native plants but not introduced species? What about a hill of grass? Which species deserve protection and which can be abandoned, left for possible extinction?

The other problem with creating a legal and ethical code as part of a renewed relationship with plants comes back to that issue of consumption. The Animal Protection Movement is a groundswell of outrage and admonishment of bad agricultural and animal husbandry practice, and the endemic negative effects of industries such as cattle production on the environment. Hence the rise in vegetarianism.

Can plants have the same rights as animals? As humans? Maybe they should disallow their own edibility. Perhaps plants should legally own the land they are rooted in. These ideas sound outrageous, but there is an implication that our human desire to own the earth is equally outrageous. Just think of how a small terrace house in Newtown, Sydney, sells for more than $3 million. The idea of moving money of that size between one another in order to call a small house on a tiny plot of land your own, becomes quite ludicrous. What do humans think they're buying?

In the landmark Australian High Court ruling *Mabo v Queensland (No 2)* that dismantled the doctrine of *terra nullius* (nobody's land) in favour of Native Title, there was an acknowledgement of different systems of law, one Indigenous, one Western. Making the two systems compatible requires thought, consideration, consultation and drafting of new legislation.

We can't do that with non-human entities such as plants, because vegetal matter can't sign contracts. It could be argued that Earth Jurisprudence (a legal system of governance that accounts for the whole earth, advocated by South African attorney Cormac Cullinan) does not act for nature at all. What the law can do is defend nature against thoughtless human acts that damage ecologies. It is still humans dealing with humans.

I hear people crying: this is too much! This is too far-fetched to suggest that nature should have its own agency! In many ways, I feel the same way. But it wasn't so long ago that animal rights were not part of mainstream cultural life. The change in attitude towards animals was quick once it gained momentum. I suspect the same advocacy will happen for the plant world.

This work is a call to arms. The 2022 federal election in Australia, where independent candidates responded to a widespread call for a better national response to climate change, show us all how important the environment is.

Why can't we care for the rivers in Australia in the same way as Whanganui? Why aren't we drawing up legislation right now to protect the plants, trees, waters and birds now? Why?

MY MOTHER AND
THE ORCHIDS

Out the front of my terrace house, I have three pots of echinopsis growing. They are tall, spiky cactus plants that look as if they may topple over at any moment. Kind of ugly, their prickles are ferocious, perhaps to make up for their less conventionally attractive form. And, yes, to deter aggressors.

But the flowers of these cacti are a different story. The flowers are completely unbelievable. First, a weird bud appears, looking like a stuffed zucchini flower, and then suddenly it just explodes into bloom. And then, just as quickly, it dies off.

It's hard to explain how striking these flowers are and I think it's because the white petals are multiple, velvety and super white. It's also because the blooms seem oversized in relation to the plant. Or maybe it's because their delicacy contrasts with the spikiness of the green stems.

So striking are they that most of my neighbours come over to photograph them. First one bud blooms and the next day it is gone. Then the next and next in daily succession. That's the other shocking thing about the echinopsis flower – it's outrageously short-lived but connected to the other plants.

This is the element of the cactus I love the most. Its fleetingness. Busy for the day? Too bad, you don't get to witness the extreme beauty of the bloom. I went away during one of its flowerings and when I came home I could see the flopped post-blooming sag of the flower. I'd missed a special event.

My mother missed an opportunity too. There was a large garden where she grew up. While my grandfather's health was poor, he had a vision. A vision for orchids.

According to my mum, my grandfather built (or had built) two large walk-in aviaries for pheasants and finches. Then a glasshouse was built, and then there were two bush houses around the lower vegetable patch. The glasshouse had fibro walls, glass panes as a roof, and inside there was a path down the centre with wooden racks on either side. One area was like a huge tray for plants that could stand in a little water. Power was connected and water too … one tap had a contraption attached which made the water come out in a mist.

The bush houses were different. They were quite simple, with a low brick support wall holding built-up soil, and a metal frame over them both to which my grandfather stapled strips of aluminium similar to that used in venetian blinds – providing some shade, but not completely. Into the bush houses he put dozens of cymbidium orchids in terracotta pots, and into the glass house went the more delicate orchids such as cattleyas. Moss grew on the ground and before long my grandmother had planted some of her beloved maidenhair fern.

My mother explains, 'We children were expected to look after the birds and to change their feed and water daily. As we grew, we also had to look after the orchids – watering, repotting, etc. My father did none of the actual work! In time, the pheasants and finches were gone, replaced with many silkies [chickens] and we loved them. One day we let them all out and had great fun getting them back into the aviaries. We got into much trouble from our parents and we did not do that again. As we grew, we all objected to being expected to do the work – my younger brother and sister were left to battle on with looking after the orchids and our mother loved giving spikes of flowers to her friends.'

There are quite of few orchids in the herbarium collection that my grandfather also grew – 164 cymbidiums and 11 cattleyas. It looks like the earliest was collected in 1884, a cymbidium from Lismore. The sheet shows a pretty despondent specimen. I'd say it's barely a specimen, it's a ten-centimetre stick with a bit of old leaf attached to the base. Poor orchid. Nothing like the exquisite spectacle of its life. Orchids were considered ornamental and rare. The truth is that most Coles and Woolworths have bucketloads of them now. This little cymbidium, given its legacy on the specimen sheet, would have been lovely when it was on the banks of the river. I can see it swaying in the breeze there, despite this unfortunate little deathly reminder of what it has become.

By the late 1960s, my grandfather's glasshouse and bush houses had become quite ramshackle. My mum remembers, years later: 'My father rang me when they were moving out of the house into a smaller flat, and said he wanted me to have the orchids. I said *no thank you* – I never wanted to see another orchid. I think I hurt his feelings quite badly. How times have changed and how I wish I had at least taken some of them!'

I understand my mother's regret. Another missed opportunity?

Perhaps we are all realising, hopefully not too late, the value of plants.

THE BANKSIA: PLANT-SPIRIT

After spending a lot of time poring over the specimens in the herbarium collection and interviewing all kinds of people about their connection to plants and how that informs the activities of the herbarium, I realised that the collection experiences often encouraged me to go and see their counterparts in nature, in the park, in the bush.

I'd been staring at and writing about the banksia tree and its controversial name, so I decided to visit a real one again. Yes, again. As I love to do. For reassurance, in some way. Maybe for connection.

The day was slightly on edge. Twitchy and unstable. It was pushed around by a warm wind and the flies were large and lazy. This was up near Port Stephens, north of Sydney. The flannel flowers had just come out and I found the *Banksia serrata* tree I knew and had seen many times before. I sat and leaned against its trunk.

The trunk of this particular tree was rough, like old crocodile skin, but I leaned back anyway and watched other bush visitors wander past. These trees really are quite funny, I thought on this spring day, like looking up at the underside of a grotesque giant. It was so heavy with its bushy flower-cones, which had darkened over recent months. Even though this tree had glossy evergreen saw-cut leaves, it still looked like its cones were too big and pendulous for its body.

The flowers on the tree I leaned against had been pollinated and the flowers were dark grey wood, rather than honey-coloured brushes. Many had opened up their seed follicles, and it looked like a hundred eyes were watching me.

I felt the tree trunk shift behind me in the breeze – a signature of these trees as they have shallow roots in sandy soil. It was the first week of October and I knew there was an extra hour of sunlight, so I felt unrushed. Perhaps the tree knew this too.

Parrots swarmed to this tree, then swarmed away. Two small wattle birds arrived and pecked at each other's beaks … quite aggressively. They flew away, returned, and fought again. This was a busy place to sit and watch, it turned out.

It was almost too windy to enjoy but I leaned back and rested. Suddenly, after five minutes of deep calm, the breeze picked up again. My banksia tree leaned sideways a centimetre or so, and then I received a hefty smack on the head, as though someone had thrown a cricket ball at me. I mean, it really hurt.

I sat forward, feeling dazed, and looked around. There were some walkers who slowed to stare at me but didn't stop. Then I noticed a huge banksia cone at my feet. It had fallen from a branch and whacked me on the head. Rubbing my crown, I leaned over and picked it up. Had it dropped from a high branch? That would explain why it hurt.

A jogger slowed to a near-but-not-total stop and called, 'That flower just dropped on your head.'

I resisted the urge to call back: 'No shit, Sherlock'. Pain makes me cranky. *And it's not a bloody flower anymore.* The cone had indeed dropped on my head and it had pulled out a tiny chunk of my curls, too, which were now attached to the cone in a nasty clump. I honestly had a throbbing headache by now, so I climbed to my feet and attempted a stalking-away from the tree.

But when I was about ten metres away, I stopped, turned and looked back at this strong and aggressive tree. Fierce is the word that came to mind. It was kind of impressive, I realised as I rubbed my head. Perhaps the tree knew that's how I saw it. Impressively ancient, sometimes menacing, and maybe not the prettiest cake in the cake shop.

Banksia serrata are memorable trees and I wish I'd kept that banksia seed cone with a chunk of my tangled hair in it as a souvenir. But my head hurt in an eye-crossing way and I was not thinking straight. My thoughts wandered.

While it is true that Western science often uncritically asserts 'discovery' of species, the importance of prior Indigenous names and knowledge systems are beginning to be recognised in recent articles published by taxonomists and ecologists.[52] I thought about that wisdom, alongside the 60 000-plus years of Indigenous wisdom that came before.

About six months later in April, I went back again to visit that rascal of a banksia tree that conked me on the head. Once bitten, twice shy, I didn't sit beneath it. Instead I walked around the tree to make sure the season was very different and there were no ugly hairy cones about to drop on my head.

I was in luck because the tree had a bouquet of creamy yellow flowers. The tree looked in fine health, without the dark cones (and its darker intentions) and without the mess they usually left at the foot of the tree. In fact, it was completely transformed, as though it were a prettier version of itself or had had a makeover.

I sat on the grass a few metres away. I realised that this tree could never have only one name. On the second visit, it was so different from its former self. Its leaves were incandescent, even the structure of the branches, without its heavy cones, looked less twisted and violent.

The tree clearly needed myriad names for its various body parts and seasonal states. I texted some friends to make some suggestions for all the different iterations that are the *Banksia serrata* and they came up with these: tough guy; hairy balls; baby bottle brush; lime splice; coin slot; dirty old man.

I chuckled at these names. But I now feel the banksia has been much-maligned. All these names are so male, so influenced by the Big Bad Banksia Men stories that May Gibbs peddled. This banksia tree, I could see, was more than one gender. Perhaps the banksia takes on whatever gender we want them to be.

Isn't she also a goddess? How fierce are her leaves and cones. How creamy her flowers. As I stared at this fierce and powerful tree, it occurred to me that she was not simply a man at all. She was a warrior. She was not conventionally beautiful. But she was bold and fiery.

I realised, as I stood staring at this fiery and sometimes brutal tree, that I'd found the plant I've been looking for. Her name, on this particular day only, was Luna. I have no idea what her name will be next time we meet.

ACKNOWLEDGEMENTS

This book was possible due to the support of the Australian Research Council. It has been more collaborative than my previous books, in both the process and in the editing. I am grateful to my son George who helped me re-order the chapters in draft one. Thank you, clever and versatile George. I then turned to my dear friend and colleague Anna Westbrook after I'd done a fair bit of rewriting. As a brilliant novelist and a scholar, she was able to see the overall structure of the book and provide coherent advice.

Then the wonderful Gillian Serisier took on the role of reader. I knew Gillian would be straight (blunt) with me. She found some thoughtless errors, some ill-considered descriptions and made some excellent suggestions. Gillian, you are also one of my hero-gardeners.

When the manuscript went to editor Linda Funnell, we worked together to remove errors and repetitions. Linda is a master artisan of words, with a keen eye for potential trouble. Thank you.

All the wonderful people I interviewed, and have quoted, were sent their chapters for checking and for correcting any errors. I'd like to thank you all for being so fascinating, so collaborative and so enthusiastic about your chapters. You are Barbara Briggs, Aunty Susan Grant, Natalie Valiente, Caine Barlow, Jonathon (Ronny) Carmichael, Liam Engel, Darklight, 'Graham' and 'James,' Cathy Offord, Claire Brandenberger, Joel Cohen, Dakota Feirer, Denise Ora, Fabri Blacklock, Aunty Zona Wilkinson, Shelley James, Graeme Errington, Hannah McPherson, John Siemon, Gerry Turpin,

Luke Patterson, John Waight, Marco Duretto, Miguel Garcia, Peter Cuneo, Steve Allsop, Sandra Davidson and Uncle Ivan Wellington. I am pleased to thank Josh Brown and Brendan Broadbent, who both worked at the Royal Botanic Garden, for advising me on Aboriginal protocol and research best practice. Special thanks to Dr Mariko Smith from the Australian Museum Sydney, for reading the entire manuscript and checking Aboriginal protocol, appropriateness and best practice for writing about these issues.

Special thanks also to Director Denise Ora and Chief Scientist Brett Summerell at the Royal Botanic Garden and Domain Trust and the Australian Institute of Botanical Science, who have been my three-year research partners on this herbarium ARC Linkage project. I have learned so much from you both that, at times, my head nearly exploded with excitement. Thanks to the University of NSW for hosting my project.

Finally, thank you to publisher Elspeth Menzies for being so open and embracing of a second book – you have a keen publishing vision and editing eye and I'm honoured to be included in that creativity. Lastly, my thanks to Deb McInnes, especially for suggesting she might need to take out extra insurance should she do publicity for this plant book.

NOTES

1. Gibson, Prudence, *The Rapture of Death*. Sydney: Boccalatte, 2010.
2. Shteir, Ann, 'Gender and "Modern" Botany in Victorian England', *Women, Gender and Science: New Directions* 12, (1997): 29–38.
3. Cook, James, *Captain Cook's Voyages of Discovery*. London: Heron Books, 1970.
4. Araluen, Evelyn, 'Snugglepot and Cuddlepie in the Ghost Gum', *Sydney Review of Books* 11 February 2019. <www.sydneyreviewofbooks.com/essay/snugglepot-and-cuddlepie-in-the-ghost-gum-evelyn-araluen>
5. Bacon, J.M., 'Settler Colonialism as eco-social structure and the production of colonial ecological violence', *Environmental Sociology* 5, 1 (2018): 63.
6. Ibid.
7. Smith, Linda Tuhiwai, *Decolonising Methodologies: Research and Indigenous People*. London: Zed, 2012.
8. Atlas of Living Australia, 'Species: Banksia Serrata' Search species. Accessed 12 August 2021. <bie.ala.org.au/species/https://id.biodiversity.org.au/taxon/apni/51293610>
9. AIATSIS, 'Map of Indigenous Australia'. Accessed 28 August 2021. <aiatsis.gov.au/explore/map-indigenous-australia>
10. Turpin, Gerry and Liz Cameron, 'Yarning up with Gerry Turpin', *Ecological Management and Restoration* 23, 1 (2022): 17–21.
11. Gibson, *The Rapture of Death*.
12. Choi, Charles, 'Caffeinated "Vomit Drink" Nauseated North America's First City', Live Science, 7 August 2012. <www.livescience.com/22136-caffeinated-black-drink-first-city.html>
13. Hemery, Gabriel, *Green Gold: The epic true story of Victorian plant hunter John Jeffrey*. London: Unbound, 2019.
14. Spjut, R., Suffness, M., Cragg, G. and Norris D., 'Mosses, Liverworts, and Hornworts Screened for Antitumor Agents', *Economic Botany* 40, 3 (1986): 310–338.
15. Sumner, Ray, 'Amalie Dietrich and the Aborigines: Her contribution to Australian anthropology and ethnography', *Australian Aboriginal Studies* (1993): 2.
16. Etheredge, George, 'Monica Gagliano: Do Plants Have Something to Say?' *New York Times*, 26 August 2019. <www.nytimes.com/2019/08/26/style/can-plants-talk.html>
17. 'Journeys in our time: Bundle', Macquarie Archives. <www.mq.edu.au/macquarie-archive/journeys/people/profiles/bundle.html>
18. Muhammed, Kahlil Gibran, 'The Barbaric History of Sugar in America', *New York Times Magazine*, 14 August 2019. <www.nytimes.com/

19. Australian Human Rights Commission, 'Australian South Sea Islanders: A century of race discrimination under Australian law (2003)'. <www.humanrights.gov.au/our-work/race-discrimination/publications/australian-south-sea-islanders-century-race>
20. 'Sugar slaves black chapter in in agricultural history', *ABC Rural*, ABC News, 30 September 2013. <www.abc.net.au/news/rural/2013-09-27/sugar-enslaveds-black-chapter-in-agricultural-history/4985102>
21. Annual Report, Guam Agricultural Experiment Station, College of Agriculture, University of Guam, 1994. <www.uog.edu/_resources/files/wptrc/1994_AES_Annual_Report.pdf>
22. Antonelli, Alexandre, 'Director of science at Kew: It's time to decolonise botanical collections', *The Conversation*, 19 June 2020. <theconversation.com/director-of-science-at-kew-its-time-to-decolonise-botanical-collections-141070>
23. Kenny, Michael, 'A Darker Shade of Green', *Social History of Medicine* 15, 3 (December 2002): 481–504.
24. Pujol, Ernesto, 'Decolonising a Caribbean Garden', *The Planthunter*, 19 August 2021. <www.theplanthunter.com.au/gardens/decolonising-a-caribbean-garden>
25. 'Sisal hemp in Fiji', *Bulletin of Miscellaneous Information*, Royal Botanic Gardens, Kew, vol 1913, 6 (1913): 231–233. <www.jstor.org/stable/4115011>
26. 'Local solutions in Fiji build agricultural research capacity amid Covid19', *Australian Centre for International Agricultural Research*, 16 July 2020. <www.aciar.gov.au/media-search/blogs/local-solutions-fiji-build-agricultural-research-capacity-amid-covid-19>
27. Schiebinger, Londa, *Plants and Empire: Colonial bioprospecting in the Atlantic world*, Cambridge: Harvard University Press, 2007, 30.
28. Casey, Scott, 'A cup of tea, a Bex and a good lie down', *Australian Pharmacist*, 12 June 2018. <www.australianpharmacist.com.au/cup-of-tea-bex-good-lie-down/>
29. 'Ask Margaret Ross', *Psychwire*, 2022. <www.psychwire.com/ask/topics/17gkejz/ask-margaret-ross-about-the-use-of-psilocybin-in-palliative-care->
30. Interview with Steve Allsop, November 2021.
31. News staff, 'Police uncover Breaking Bad-style lab allegedly run by mum with cancer in Western Australia', Nine News, 15 June 2020. <www.9news.com.au/national/perth-news-drugs-lab-mum-with-cancer-breaking-bad-police/aba9e86c-3cfd-4086-b06c-c103b7055954>
32. Orsolini, L. et al., 'How does ayahuasca work from a psychiatric perspective? Pros and cons of the entheogenic therapy', *Hum Psychopharmacol* 35, 3 (2020): e2728. <www.pubmed.ncbi.nlm.nih.gov/32220028/>

33 Voogelbreinder, Snu, 'Psychoactive Australian Acacia species and their alkaloids', YouTube, 5 July 2018. <www.youtube.com/watch?v=X4gcKm8TgZU>
34 Hente, Corinna, 'Golden wattle, more than just a pretty flower', *Mojo News*, 5 September 2014. <www.mojonews.com.au/page/golden-wattle-more-than-just-a-pretty-flower>
35 Sarhangi, Sheila, 'Bishop Museum Botanist finds undiscovered plants in Papua New Guinea', *Honolulu Magazine* 11 June 2012. <www.honolulumagazine.com/bishop-museum-botanist-finds-undiscovered-plants-in-papua-new-guinea/>
36 Lydon, Jane, 'Grappling with Australia's Legacy of Slavery', University of Western Australia, 9 July 2021. <www.uwa.edu.au/news/article/2021/july/grappling-with-australias-legacies-of-slavery>
37 National Herbarium of New South Wales, Sydney Botanic Gardens, Sydney.
38 Antonelli, Alexandre, 'Our Manifesto for Change 2021–2030'. <www.kew.org/about-us/press-media/manifesto-for-change-2021> Antonelli, Alexandre, 'It's time to decolonise botanical collections', *The Conversation*, 9 June 2020. <theconversation.com/director-of-science-at-kew-its-time-to-decolonise-botanical-collections-141070>
39 MacPhail, Mike, 'A Hidden Cultural Landscape: Colonial Sydney's Plant Microfossil Record', *Australian Historical Archaeology* 17, 1999. <www.jstor.org/stable/29544433>
40 Nargi, Lela, 'The Miyawaki Method: A better way to build forests?', *JSTOR Daily*, 24 July 2019. <www.daily.jstor.org/the-miyawaki-method-a-better-way-to-build-forests/>
41 Papers of Dymphna Clark, MS 9873, Series 6. <www.nla.gov.au/nla.obj-415222454/findingaid>
42 Ibid.
43 Interview with Gordon Guymer, Brisbane Herbarium, 29 November, 2017.
44 Christopher, Ian, 'The plant that killed Socrates,' *Medium*, 14 June 2020. <www.medium.com/illumination/the-plant-that-killed-socrates-cd45b63a06c2>
45 Defossez, Emmanuel et al., 'Ant plants and fungi: A new three way symbiosis', *New Phytologist* 182, 4 (2009): 942–949.
46 Ibid.
47 Sheldrake, Merlin, *Entangled Life*. Sydney: Penguin, 2020, 5.
48 Ibid., 234.
49 Gibson, *The Rapture of Death*.
50 Brazier, Jan and Duggins, Molly, 'Visualising Nature: Models and wall charts for teaching biology in Australia and New Zealand', *National Museum of Australia* 10, 2. <www.recollections.nma.gov.au/issues/volume_10_number_2/papers/visualising_nature>

51　University of Tokyo, 'Plants can smell, now researchers know how', *Science Daily*, 23 January 2019. <www.sciencedaily.com/releases/2019/01/190123105827.htm>

52　Wehi, Priscilla M., Brownstein, Gretchen and Morgan-Richards, Mary, 'Indigenous plant naming and experimentation reveal a plant-insect relationship in New Zealand forests', *Conservation Science and Practice*, 2 (2020): e282.

Trisos, Christopher H., Auerbach, Jess and Katti, Madhusudan, 'Decoloniality and anti-oppressive practices for a more ethical ecology', *Nature Ecology & Evolution*, 5 (2021): 1205–1212.

Knapp, Sandra, Vorontsova, Maria S. and Turland, Nicholas J., 'Indigenous Species Names in Algae, Fungi and Plants: A Comment on Gillman & Wright', *Taxon*, (31 December 2020): 1409–1410.